SHAVING

STEPHEN BERG

FOUR WAY BOOKS / *Marshfield*

Library of Congress Number 96-61434
ISBN 1-884800-17-3, cloth
ISBN 1-884800-14-9, paper

Manufactured in the United States of America on acid free paper.

Design: Cynthia Krupat
Production: Acme Art, Inc.
Printing: McNaughton and Gunn

Four Way Books is a division of Friends of Writers, Inc., a Vermont-based not-for-profit organization.
We are grateful for the assistance we receive from individual donors and private foundations.

Some of these pieces, in earlier versions, have appeared in *The Colorado Review, The Denver Quarterly, The Kenyon Review, The Threepenny Review, TriQuarterly,* and *New and Selected Poems,* published by Copper Canyon Press.

To Michael Ryan

Contents

e se pensassi come, al vostro guizzo,
guizzo dentro a lo specchio vostra image,
ciò che par duro ti parrebbe vizzo.

from Canto XXV, *Purgatorio,* Dante

It doesn't even matter who we are, all three of us, sitting in the living room of a house in a city—a sick old dying man, a woman, a younger man—arguing over what the sick one wants to leave, to whom, after he's dead. The man and wife sit in front of a bookcase wall. He's almost dead from a massive coronary. She's half-hysterical. The other man's their son, and he's half-nuts from the sickness and the craziness, from how this moment resurrects an entire family history by condensing it, a primal myth, without imagery from the past, into one room, one time, forever, *forever*, the young man thinks, although he has no memory of other incidents like this, of a mad trio hacking out of their souls sheer loveless misery, so pure it could pose as joy or ecstasy, its singleness of purpose like one of those celebrated Tudor lyrics organized to perfect an argument by coiling it tight around a single image, theme or idea. The drama here is after-death, or whatever term is right for the near-dead writing a will after waiting a lifetime, not consulting his heirs, too ill now to think straight, too terrified to know what he feels about "his loved ones," who should get what—the car, the tiny row house, money from a policy or two—all an ambitious businessman, who didn't really make it, has to leave them. The sick man has never admitted he might actually die. The woman has always worried that she would wind up with nothing, has always felt she had nothing, or less, or not enough. It's impossible to describe the scar on her mind. The air in the room is like old unventilated sweat now. The man, in his faded blue and white striped bathrobe, balances a pad of yellow lined paper on his knee with his right hand, a pencil hung between two fingers like an unlit cigarette. Meanwhile the parents are chattering about the young man (in his late thirties) and what he should get. "He shouldn't be able to sell anything until he's 55," the woman barks. "He'll be a big boy, someday," squeaks the old man, an insane, hostile remark, the young man thinks, knowing he has heard a sentence from his father that will fester permanently. Finally, the yellow sheet has writing all over it and the woman is satisfied. The young man, who feels like a weary, abused boy now, hates them both. Three weeks later the man dies. The woman gets what she wants, what there is, although she never forgives the man for—it doesn't matter. The identities of the people do not matter, as I've said, because, as the years pass, in the mind, it all becomes the person in whose mind it lives. The only salvation for certain minds is if they believe death destroys everything that was there, in the mind, believe immortality beyond mind doesn't exist—unless one tells in vivid detail the story to someone else, so it becomes part of another mind. But that's mere theory. On the bookshelf, a few inches above those two aging heads—Zola's *Nana*, in a cheap paper binding, several pages still stuck together at erratic spots, six or seven sepia photographic likenesses on slick paper of Nana, in different naked poses, a man's head plunged between her breasts; lying on a couch; standing, nipples stiff and pink, semi-profile. Exciting, but as a boy I loved the sex passages more, where the couple is described staring at each other undressing or fondling each other or doing strange oral things. Day after day, I'd stretch out on the sofa, stand the book on my chest, holding it with my left hand, and, just before I'd come, slip the book down, then close the book and put it back on the shelf, hoping they'd take out the book someday, pull apart those pages, know me.

Three weeks before he died, my father acted as an extra in *A New Leaf*, a movie about an alcoholic, her lover, and a stranger who showed up and would, as it happened, try to save her. Cassavetes and May were making the film in Philly on 13th Street, using a defunct hotel, renamed *The Royal*, for the battles between the screwed-up couple. Night after night the crew would take their places—at the camera, yelling directions, searching for extras in the crowds lined up six deep around the roped-off set to watch Peter Falk (the stranger) do a scene in which he's passing *The Royal* on his way somewhere and a whiskey bottle flies out a window and hits the ground at his feet and he looks up, sees someone (the woman, I think) in the window and dashes (there's a scream) into the dark building. It seems the woman and her lover (Cassavetes) are holed-up there, planning a robbery. Falk is tanned, dressed in a custom-cut Navy-blue silk suit and delicate black shoes, Italian style, like the ones tap dancers use because they're so flexible, nearly weight-less. In and out, in and out he goes, repeating the scene, bottle after bottle arcing from the window, the pieces swept away each time by one of the crew, while none of the fans and gawkers really knows what the story is. It was like watching real life, it doesn't matter whose life, with one big difference: shot so many times, that scene lost all meaning. It was starting to get hot the way it does in Philly in early June—thick greasy humid air, hanging on for days so every little thing feels difficult, everything looks like it has sweat and grime on it. My father had had a massive, fifth heart attack and when we picked him up at his house he was wearing a raincoat, single-breasted with a full button-in camel's-hair liner, and under it a suit, tie and scarf. A gray felt hat and gray doeskin gloves lent the finishing touches. His face was the color of those gloves, it had a dull shine like solder, like those Philly skies before a rain when blossoming puffs of air cool your face but it stays hot, the sun has disappeared, everything is drained of strong color. Well, he walked, shuffling one foot at a time very very slowly, stopping between each step, as if on a tightrope, almost floating, with great caution and weakness and fear, to the car. Settled in the front seat, he barely spoke. We heard the movie was being made, thought it would be fun to watch the production, a rare distraction from all he had gone through, drove the few blocks to the place, parked, walked over to the people at the ropes circling *The Royal*, and faded into the crowd. My Dad, for some reason, drifted to another side of the crowd and stood at the back of it. Everything on the street was blue-white under the lights; the mist of humidity in the glare put a fine pearly veil between you and whatever you saw. Once in a while I'd glance around to see how he was. Inch by inch he had slipped through the mob until now he was standing up front pressing against the waist-high rope—all gray: raincoat, gloves, hat, face. Except for his Watch-plaid cashmere scarf. He looked like a Mafia Don: implacable mask of a face, a man with secrets and power who refused the world any hint of emotion that might reveal who he was. Was his mind silent as he stood there or did he hear one of those primitive, sourceless, pure, self-defining voices that haunt us, left over from the gods, telling him not to smile, not to speak, not to show anything to the enemy world, telling him to be no one as the line between death and the future evaporated and he edged closer to the playground of the gods by obeying them, by adopting the hero's impassive mask? The fact is he looked like Edward G. Robinson, not Oedipus or Lear immortalized in the revelatory aftermath of cosmic self-discovery. Reticent, masochistic, mildly depressed all his life, he stood there, to me awesome because of his courage near death. "He'll never walk out of the hospital," the doctor had said, and five months later, here he was, as fate would have it, a passerby about to act in a bad movie, about to play one of the gods as they are today. By now

Elaine May was pacing the edge of the crowd inside the roped-off area, looking for extras, picking people by their faces to walk past under an arcade twenty or so feet behind Falk during the bottle-throwing scene. She saw my father, nodded a questioning "Yes?" He ducked under the rope, which May lifted for him, and joined a group of eight on the edge of the crowd. By now I was standing beside him, listening. All were told to begin walking, briskly, scattered apart, just before Falk reaches the front of the hotel when the bottle hits. Over and over he did it, briskly, until we thought he would drop dead. Over and over I watched his speechless face, betraying nothing, glistening under his hat in the lights, while behind me, off to my right—where the camera was, pointed away from the hotel at Falk and the extras walking by—Falk ran past into the hotel, yelling something, after the bottle crashed, and a woman yelled back at him from the window. Over and over. Finally they got it right and we went home. For months, I waited for the newspaper ads announcing the film so we could see it. When it finally played, and we went, the scene wasn't even in it. The film was so mediocre it ran less than a week. I tried buying a copy of the scene but they wouldn't sell the footage. Many years since your walk-on part, and it happens anytime: the muggy summer night, the family, gauzy air, you doing what you're told by the director— I'll be teaching, washing dishes, reading, writing, talking with Millie and the kids, a middle-aged man, your son, watching his sick father, but not on the screen in a theater. It's still the street, the unknown people, you doing it over and over, over and over the scene being shot, the bottle, the scream, the lights, "Okay—try it again!" coming from behind lights and faceless faces, from behind the black steel bodies and silent blank lenses of the weapon-like cameras pointed at us.

"O siempre, nunca dar con el jamas de tanto siempre!"

—Valléjo

A phone call from my mother, screaming, "I can't wake him up!"
Throw on my clothes, leave the motel for their place. My parents'
bedroom, Longport, N.J.—summer, early dawn, before the mind
has a chance to let its own light merge with the world's, before
dreams have resolved their bright, disconnected streaks and traces
into a semblance of story. A dead body. My father's. Those sentences:
as if my father and his body had become two separate things, and
always had been, but not clearly until now. The way we think of
ourselves, like that. The fact of the dead body of my father. No words.
Not a fart or a tune or a single dribbly tear, not a peep, not that
ordinary-when-he-lived, now-so-wonderful, "How are you, son?"
just this shockingly heavy, God! immovable corpse with bluish gray-
green patches on its free arm and visible cheek, lying on its side—
Dad, you look asleep! Hey! You really look only asleep!—the poor
thing's eyes lightless behind stiff half-open lids, a brown bottle on
the floor, tiny white pills scattered like seeds, as I grab your shoulder,
Dad, knowing you're dead, and shake you and feel what "dead
weight" really means: you barely can be moved as I try to shake you
because maybe you are asleep and if it weren't for the bedsprings
you'd be a statue made of plaster or wood and only a kick in the ass
could move you. I go over and close the door and drag a chair up to
the bed and sit and look at you. Behind me, the sea pushes and slides,
as always. There's a black sack, somewhere, in a book, in my mind,
with a man in it, waiting. It flashes up. It flashes past me. He will
be in it, soon, to struggle with his dying into the light until he
discovers there is no death. But there's no boundary to consciousness,
so deep in every direction it extends. Mind like smoke, Heraclitus
says, less mass than anything, always in motion, and only movement
can know movement. Corpse. The solidity of the dead though they
can't give orders, or see, or pay bills, or fuck. O no more fucking and
eating! No more love! Each sleeper in a world of his own, each

sharing this world when awake. Dawn glazes the room. Pale grainy blue, unconsoling, tenacious as it finds an ashtray, wallet, mirror, rug, face, doorknob, ring of keys, even the blind eyes of the dead man. Us. Light. His face still pointing on its side toward the window and the sea, not seeing, not anything, not, a tiny dot of blood seeping from his lips onto the pillow. I bend over, fingertip-touch his cheek. Real. Really dead. I clutch his shoulder again to see what he weighs, to move him. I know I stroke his brow—God forgive me, I think of patting a dog—stroke it perhaps to say I understand what it is to have gone through this, to have achieved such unrewardable dignity. Which is, of course, nonsense. To help my helplessness. But to attempt to love someone after his death in the belief—it can only be belief—that love penetrates death, and is stronger, as it is in life when we love and feel time snag itself on a faucet, chair, cup, in those moments of love when we're so fully here that the "I" flares into non-existence—gone into others and objects. I touch his pajama sleeve, I know I do. I know it. Something is happening to knowing, to being conscious. It is daylight. It is The Real. I know it: yes. "One must talk about everything according to its nature, how it comes to be and how it grows." I am trying. "Men have talked about the world without paying attention to the world or to their own minds as if they were asleep or absent-minded." Of course I'm referring to myself, I want to talk about this, but I'm not even sure what this is. I know—back there now again—that I sat there for a time, though I can't remember saying one word except for a sentence (which must have been the first before all the others)—I know I spoke for awhile, but it's as if it happened in sleep or not at all, no evidence to prove it, not a shred within reach. Talking to a corpse is, no doubt, ridiculous. And the room, I remember this much, the corpse, my not-so-very-old, old Dad, the room, simply disappeared for a long long moment. A moment which began with a dreadful, accusatory breach of courtesy from my mouth—so much a sign of the music of broken love—"Oh. . .you goddam sonofabitch!" This is the threshold of not knowing and of having to know: what came out of my mouth, sitting beside his body—merely one burst, one introductory soulful song, after which it's a blank. The night before he died I was lying in bed with my wife and daughters watching TV in the motel room at the beach half a block away from where he and my mother vacation in summer. At about 10, a knock—my father, walking the dog, my mother's peewee black poodle. He wants to say goodnight. I'm too lazy, too worn out from the months of his dying, to get up and go to the door and say goodnight. Maybe I think "He's lived this long, what's one more night?" But he didn't live one more night. He died in his sleep. I see that room and his body, me leaning over him, and it's a white blank. And in between, the grief-song of nobody-knows-who, the flank of the blank sea glittering, behind me. Then the door buzzer's whine and in walks the county corpse-carrier with his thick brown canvas sack, and in he goes to the bedroom (I've stepped out) where he stays for a minute, then out he comes shouldering the body inside the sack, closed at one end by a thick glistening grin of steel zipper, walks out the door and I go back into the bedroom, close the door and sit there, God knows how long, in the echo of soliloquy. I remember at one point, before he was bagged and carried off, I placed my ear very slowly, lightly against his chest, after I undid the top button on his pajama shirt, and waited and heard absolutely nothing, nothing, then the word "genital" shook my head, and I pictured my father's cock under the sheets, limp, dribbling, gray. This abyss: no sound for a moment: then the bare sea at my back, meekly whispering, my old man, half a foot away, face blotchy, useless hands, looking as if the cold black slit between his lips might speak, as if he were searching for a word, the blind, irrelevant sun pouring itself out, on him, on us, on the walls.

The blind black chair caner is leaning still against the Fidelity Bank building on 16th Street in Philly where I live, a 2x2 inch hunk of woven cane pinned on his lapel with a safety pin to advertise his trade, a dented tin cup drooping, hooked on his left hand's index finger, a beach chair, its green crisscross webbing, dangerously frayed, open behind him in the doorway. Most of the time he keeps one leg bent back, foot against the wall; a lunch bag sits, usually, rolled closed on the ground; passing him mornings I'll drop a coin in and hear "Thank you." About six years ago after my father died, cleaning out a closet, I found his brand-new single breasted charcoal-gray Tripler overcoat draped on a hanger. When the nap caught the light it glowed like pollen on a flower petal; the dull black bone buttons shone; the irregular deeply notched narrow lapels were hand-cut and -sewn. I'd wear it now and then but my father was short, it stopped above my knees, my jacket and shirtsleeves would show, the armpits were tight and high. Even in daylight the weave was almost invisible. It had a tricky black-on-black pattern: each sixteenth of an inch something like a tiny dim snowflake or a minuscule ghost face appeared, but you couldn't see the flakes or the faces unless you stood nose to the coat and squinted and focused and told yourself you were actually seeing those things, actually looking at that faint grid of signs, that mesmerizing text that might be some unfathomable spiritual message or a field of code as indecipherable as the self. I remember looking into a mirror once, not knowing who I was, the face in the glass seemed not to be my face, disconnected from any knowledge of whose it was, the way a word can lose its meaning if you repeat it enough times, or an object seem uncanny if you keep staring at it. It was the morning after I decided to quit therapy, "give myself a Christmas present," I announced to my shrink. I woke scared, I didn't know why, and at the sink when I wet my beard and looked up to shave, lifting my soapy hands, I didn't recognize myself, I felt I didn't exist, the face was flat, distant, a stranger's—". . .a sudden inward flash. . ."—emptiness. When I went to the closet all there was was the thick fine wool, smelling a little of damp and dust, and me, staring at the coat, almost merged with the dark inside the closet: acidic whiffs of old rubber boots and the musk of scarves and gloves floated out: the body of my father, dressed in his coat, in the grainy gray smoke-hazed lowlit air of Jimmy Ryan's, New York—one winter night I took him there to hear some of the jazz I love: my father and I sitting across from each other in the dense light: now and then a word, a sentence: his drumming fingers. It was snowing that night as it was when I stared into the closet at his coat, carried it downtown and gave it to the black man, draped it over his arm, neatly folded, told him it had been my father's—they were about the same size—and he held the coat, tenderly, folded over his right arm while, face to face, we waited in silence, me, tiny, standing in the black lenses of his glasses. "Thank you. . .Thank you. . ." he intoned, finally, in a soft gentle-manly voice, and I left. Next day, instead of his flimsy raincoat, he wore my father's coat. It was still snowing. I walked past without speaking, kept my eyes half-closed against the big sloppy flakes—unascending hymns to lost love: phrases, chords, pieces of stories that have nothing to do with coats, pity, blindness, word-static, ripped through my head—turned right off 16th up Walnut, my image in the store windows appearing, disappearing between metal and stone, and heard, "If you were here, if you. . ."—whoever the *you* is.

Could it be they are here with us but in a form we refuse to recognize since everything has to be physical to us, or it isn't real, everything has to be edible, beautiful, visible, could it be those lost beloved voices, transparent as air itself, are singing songs silent only to consciousness, to us, the living? A friend talks about looking at a photograph of his dead father, and "how partial, how unfinished" life seems to be, "a terrible sense of incompleteness" when he sees his Dad's seventy-year-old eyes watching him from the glossy grays of the snapshot, perhaps beckoning, perhaps merely observing, perhaps questioning, perhaps bestowing a grace. I remember when he told me his father had cancer and then, months after, he'd report amazing little scenes among the family at home or in the hospital, his father always the warrior, always the man face to face with his dying, uncomplaining except in one almost god-like way, in one absolutely precise, heroic deed that makes me shiver with gratitude. One day, my friend called and told me his father, the night before, after a month of incredible pain, looked up at him and said, in a fierce whisper, "It's taking too long!" No fear, according to my friend, no tone of whining or inadequacy. I said, "Jesus, that's amazing!" And he said, "Well, you know, my father always thought he was right about everything." Isn't it true that being here actually is what Zen priest Ikkyū meant when he gave himself the name Ikkyū? The word means "a pause," and maybe my friend's father knew that, had become that. Maybe that's what being right was, to him. I can imagine the man, dead now, yes, but present, somehow here, all incompleteness gone in the next, immeasurable phase of his being in absence.

It comes back often when it snows or when it's cold—the cheap marbleized shiny deep blue linoleum "rug" my folks bought for my bedroom instead of a wool rug, two wide yellow and red bands about an inch apart decorating the edge, which almost touched the walls. It never seemed clean because, when the dawn sun slanted across it so it glowed, you'd see dust, the gauziest layer, you could always pick out scuffs and smears dulling the waxed surface. I never could get used to it. It was scary at night, like having heaven for the floor of your own room. Isn't that crazy? Think of it—you're about eight, lying in bed, lost, listening to Jack Benny or Sky King materialize from behind the brown plastic fins masking the speaker of the radio, rapt in those programs and the ceiling, the known limit of a ceiling, its glass-hatted fixture glistening in the center, bursts of canned laughter, King's engine gunning, Benny's plaintive wry ingenuous "Raah-chester. . .", and you envision infinity beneath you, you see what you'll step into if you need to pee or want to raid the refriger-ator. On braver nights, you lie there, tuning out the world, door closed, the sky-floor all around you, in a bed, in the universe, not yet free enough to plummet or float through space that has no begin-ning or end, no objects, nothing to stop you: then, you peer over the bedside, once, twice, and stare hard and make out flecks of indefinite color beckoning, convinced they are stars, stars just beginning to reach us or stars so young they barely can be seen.

Blue vapor tinting the air, musky September night, houses, sycamores peeling, scrolled dry brown leaves, garbage stacked for collection, the evening doused with sickly lush autumnal breaths, garish chill of the lamps. In my house there's a party going on, nearly a hundred guests celebrating my mother's 70th; in my house, I'm amazed that I live—furniture, a dog, two lovely daughters, good wife, stereo, planted yard—all the amenities of the middle class ensconced in an up-and-coming neighborhood owned first by merchants, let slide, inhabited now by Puerto Ricans tinkering their jacked-up cars, dancing outside in the mild air: the common insatiable push upward through the ruins of the poor. People are dancing in my house, and drinking, talking and laughing, people are sitting and standing. She's cross-legged on the floor, next to me; I sit above her in a chair. Everything's faintly ominous as it always is when my mother visits. A long dark pause. I hear her reply (to whose words, I don't know) "You can't depend on Steve. . .for anything." Whispered, but loud enough so I'll hear. Then I lean down a little, and say just loud enough so she'll hear, "Mother. . .go to hell." Earlier, drunk, she had carried part of her cake into the street and called several kids over under a lamp to share it. From our steps I could see them down the block, squatting in the blue haze as she scooped out chunks with her hands and plopped the chocolatey stuff into their cupped hands. They were laughing. They were loving it. "Take! Take!" she yelled. It had such a mad eerie look to it, so out of context you couldn't tell if it was sick or saintly, public or private, it seemed an act of freedom beyond the ordinary—confession, vacation trips, lies, making money, sex—a vision of the spiritual. Then she returned, washed her hands, rejoined the party. And now she rises from the floor, beside me, disappears. A silence I recognize, a root of terror in my life, seethes in the air—something like a revenge of absence or threat expressed through a god's refusal to explain why what is is what it is. In a minute she's at the door, trying to unlock it with the key that's always in the lock but our door's old, difficult to lock and unlock, unless you're familiar with it, she stands there, smashed, trapped, furious, unable to twist the key and withdraw the deadbolt from its slot, she tries to open it for at least five minutes and then starts screaming, "Let me out!" locked in this house with all these people, yelling louder and louder, until suddenly it opens and she rushes into the street. Sometimes, on glorious nights, I step out back to follow the stars, blankly, without a thought, without names, without a crumb of understanding left to interfere, to console, and listen, and look up with the pure true gaze of an animal.

Nothing reveals enough, no wisdom consoles our ghostliness, our carnal incompleteness, our flesh speaking to mind, mind arguing with flesh in skirmishes of soul grappling with its inaccessible unity. "I like to think of myself as a woman./Here in my house, where I am/The mother of children, while my/Husband sleeps—Here in the light/Of the moon's fullness, I hear/An owl lamenting from/ The trees who creeps up closer and closer/to me in the dark. Between the two lights/of dusk and dawn. I see."—the voice of an unknown woman scribbled on the inside back cover of a copy of Neumann's *Amor and Psyche* in tentative delicate ballpoint, a few words crossed out. She wrote it for herself, I guess, then sold the book to a bookseller, who put it on a shelf or an outdoor stall, and I bought it. For years I didn't see it. I knew the quote at the back was there, but I didn't really read it until now. Not that I'm different now, but something seems to have changed. No special love, no fear, no yoke of longing, no despair; there's a transparent freshness over everything, the air looks absolutely clear, a body in itself that needs no solidity to exist. In the book, in a section about the strength of the male and female egos, Neumann claims, "At the outset of every labor Psyche is overcome by a despair in which suicide seems to be the only solution." Sometimes, in the dark, alone, I find myself searching for the room in my mind where I can have what I want, not with any woman, but with one who holds me by listening in a particular way. Remembering this, imagining it, just now, starts a traumatic sadness, a nameless loss I'm unprepared for, my arms shiver as I write—a strangely fragile acceptance, imperceptible, faint syllables, traces of a porch, a beach, an embodiment of closeness, pangs of desire, odors of skin and hair.

So many years ago I can barely recall what we said or felt, we spent twenty hours on the train to Clemson speeding to your father's funeral, snuggled into a roomette like kids off on their first trip alone, on some obscure forbidden adventure that would end with us sitting in front of a hole in the ground, listening to the preacher, watching the coffin eased down by four men handling the ropes, driving back to the house for food and drink and silly-serious talk of the beloved dead man whose soul—according to your brother-in-law—was already in Heaven listening to us. He was our first parent to die. I felt safe, lounging in our tiny cave, talking, watching the scenery, eating sandwich halves and grapes. But that night on the train, awake in the top bunk, I began to feel an openness, a tenderness, the birth of a second body, a kind of transparency permeating me: every darkened detail of the cubicle, every shadowy ill-lighted blur flitting across the compartment window, radiant with perfection, with—I don't know how else to say it—eternity, undying measureless beauty. I loved everything, scared, lying there while this new thing emerged, but I didn't wake you or analyze it, I didn't try to drive it away by thinking of something else. An hour later it was gone. I climbed down the five-runged wooden ladder, groped for my suitcase, opened it and felt around for the bottle of Scotch I had packed, unscrewed the cap and sat on the suitcase in front of the glazed window, shade up, taking short sips, staring into the black landscape. The last few houselights were on, the train clacked over the rails at ninety miles an hour. We were chopping through desolation: no people, then a knot of houses; then nothing but the image of my face; then blocks of dim factories, a farm, shacks, car wrecks—things close whipping by, things in the distance drifting away—everything thinned out, cut off from us. It was like floating in the sky. Not even loneliness or death mattered, not even the recurrent suffering mind that has no cause or name. I can still see my spectral, hunched-over shape, shimmering in the bottom of the window, peering back at me through the lens of the half-empty bottle's amber. And next to me, a foot or two away, your sleeping face behind the bars of the ladder picked up light and lost light each time a train hurtled by or we passed a station or town, your dark bulk shifting now and then under the sheets, emitting toneless speech-like shards so detached from time and place I thought a god was trying to break through and speak to me with your lips.

My wife hung it there, on the wall on the way to our bedroom. When you take the five steps up to the landing in front of our door, it's on your left, usually in shadow in a gold-rimmed, oval mat, Victorian oval walnut frame, the eyes already hurt, defensive but "open," in beseeching, stunned wariness. No steadiness, no self-assurance, no clarity of mind, influence the face. The thick brown hair is mine, but the mouth is all anonymous wonder in a sullen trance and begs not to be punished. He fears the world can kill him, and will; the world is mysterious, like disease. Being alone assails him inside and out, he can't escape it, there's no courage of acceptance in his gaze, no ease at being himself. Someone has dressed him in a shirt: large white floppy Tudor collar, fringed with lace. Looking at it, at my age, I've come to believe that my mother, early in my life, a woman baffled by her pain, found my helplessness too much like her own to allow her simply to reflect my emerging self. And, sometimes, a mother even wants to kill her child so she can be free. Isn't that what our first taste of death is—invasion by another's pain, fantasy of causing that pain and not being able to stop it? Isn't that how we first split ourselves into good and bad? Example: her long red nails clawing the back of my neck one contextless afternoon in an explosion of rage and hatred, caused by I can't remember what, like a bird of prey sinking its talons. Oh, think of an awareness that lets you act without even a hint of sensing others watch you, judge you, worry about you, so that desire and action fuse—no gap, no pained self-consciousness to thwart you. What I'm getting at, what brings that formal portrait back to stir me, is the gnawing aloneness of people, of all things, of consciousness itself, and the opposite—we live in others' minds, they live in ours, sometimes flaring in images, sometimes dying to inscribe each other's flesh on ours. Each night, before I go to bed, I pass myself on the stairs, caught with an early madness spoiling my face, and, it seems, as I tuck myself in, trying not to be seen or heard, that the wild universe, out to the farthest unseen star, breathes next to me in our bed—everything flows from it, everything returns.

Nobody is punished here by someone else, there's only powdered coffee, a puddle of dogpiss soaking the floor, plates specked with last night's food, pots, pans, glasses and cups and cookbooks, broken dishwasher, cards pinned by magnets to the freezer door, white dog hair clumped in corners, the *tickatick tickatick tickatick* of its thick uncut nails hitting bare floorboards. Nobody punishes anyone but himself these days of our godlessness, our lack of faith. "God is in the pain of our fear of death," Shastov rails in *The Possessed*, calling to us—less dazed by illusion than any, more brilliant than any, his embrace of "the groundlessness of our believing" cleansing our minds. The dog stops, sits, brushes its tail against the floor, looks up, begs for bread, its customary morning snack, and snaps up a chunk the man throws to him. The man wears beltless brown corduroys, the black cotton turtleneck he slept in, stands barefoot in loafers at the kitchen counter waiting for water to boil. His cup is spooned with Nescafé. The sky looks like rain. Through the double doors to the yard—clusters of bright green shoots an inch or so high, sword tips, moss filming the side of a rock he planted, soft luminous green. All this time some kind of punishment occurs, from the moment he woke he felt it, a burning denunciation, remorse so poisonous he can't simply toss it off, analyze it, resolve it. It doesn't have a name yet; if it did he'd understand it, bury the pain with theory. This way it's threateningly more real, much worse than that famous "ordinary human unhappiness" Freud soothed us with as our condition, our normalcy, for him the point spirit-as-consciousness must reach. He pours water into a mug stencilled with happy bears sitting and standing in a daisy chain; for a minute the water boiling and the steam please him. Then it comes back—first, waking at three in fear of his hatred after their battle last night; second, the fight itself, and their desire to keep it going. It's that fear-connected-to-desire he wants to comprehend. They were at an acquaintance's art show, sculpture, mostly phallic or obvious fuckforms, wedges penetrating soft wood globes, doughnuts on spikes, tongues entering holes, that dillentantish, stupid symbolic-abstract mode people insincerely praise but don't buy. At home, afterwards, he needs talk. "Pathetic. . . ." she says, "for a 60-year-old man to do that kind of thing!" "What's pathetic about enjoying sex?" he says. "I didn't mean that . . . I meant—to make so much of it." "Bullshit. It's bad art, but at least the guy's happy about his sex life." And on and on, of course. You know the details, you know, of course, or suspect, this must have happened hundreds of times before. How else could they do it so well, know all the tricks and uses of the tricks without being terrified. No terror now. Something else, worse: Hell as not being able to be together except like this, and in his mind, out of conscious sight, time fixed in replicas of each of them at critical stages of the past, about 20 little white plaster statues of them—each with its own expression on its face, representing offenses, crimes, wrongs, the "negative"—as each soul's lived it—one by one on steps leading down into an abyss of redemptions based on their need to find salvation in the other. But the kitchen is where he is, and where they were last night. He hears her now, padding downstairs, and winces, and has a wish, and when she appears in the kitchen he reaches out and smiles, tenderness in his recognition, forgiveness, the wish to be forgiven, and asks, "Do you want some coffee? I'll make it." "No, I make it the way I like it." Of course. Of course. Like children. Christ, we were lucky, in childhood, to have wishes that couldn't come true, to have tears. Hell, then, was learning you couldn't always have what you wanted, and, slowly but surely, defining life as compromise, not as this endless woe. He stands there, next to her, watching her make her coffee. Immense silence rises from the end of the flight of statues going down, like thickening heavy smoke. His head throbs. It must be something like a stroke, he thinks.

Sentence by sentence, day by day, what he knows accumulates, continues to be heard, inside, on an invisible stage of selves all talking at once, and he can't comprehend any of it.

All through childhood I never could quite find a place in my family
where I fit, at least that's how it feels to me now when I try to see
what it was like in our house—a grandfather dying of heart disease,
grandmother, mother, father, no brothers or sisters—what it was
like to be my mother's obsession. It isn't that I can say what act, habit
or word injured me, exactly: I was who I was only through her eyes.
Her overprotective, phobic love stunned me with fear. My rowhouse
was an only child's cocoon that hummed with argument or silence.
I can't find myself at the table with family, at a movie with grown-
ups. So few clear details substantiate my time there, I can't believe
I ate, talked, slept, was a son, a little boy wishboning his pet terrier's
hind legs until she'd yelp. I'd see a baby in a carriage and hate it,
but I couldn't see my own, new, mutilated soul and stop myself. I do
see one terrifying dawn when I was five and had just waked: I lifted
my head off the pillow and looked past my feet where a huge blue
human torso, no face, no fingers, legs or hair, hung in the window
for a minute like a clump of mist, evaporated and left me shaken.
What did it mean? Who was I except someone others saw? But that's
only part of the story. Looking back, everything's either baseball
with other kids, scooping ice daggers like glass arrowheads off the
back of the truck and sucking them, step ball, sledding; everything's
outside, in the street, a vacant lot, an alley, except for a few bare
images soaked in the gloom of home. With friends I fit, with them
I could do anything, I believed, and not be watched and judged, not
be the boy whose life his mother feared for. The one I remember
best today had had polio and walked with a stiff limp, his right leg
seemed to be locked or frozen straight, his right arm hung perpetu-
ally bent, the hand had that curl-claw affliction that made flipping
pages or picking up small things or shaking hands difficult. But he
seemed to have been sweetened by the disease, by his parents'
acceptance and love. When they were there you could sense the

depth of their hovering, light smiles on their faces, bent forward a bit in an always eager readiness to help, to serve, to replace what that sick twist of fate had done to him with toy after expensive toy, games, athletic equipment, records, books, even a commercial pinball machine that stood plugged in all day and all night (he told me) in a corner of his bedroom, its waiting, glowing, glassed-in field of slots and tinted bumpers, its scoreboard splashed with monsters, war scenes, planes and tanks, invectives branding the red air between the creatures spewed from their mouths, all as if sent up from some hellish abyss. It stood there like a sentinel guarding the gates to another life, a life I had no inkling of, beneath this life, always beneath this life, a life later I wanted and feared, the place in the mind where truth was. A huge toybox in his room was always open when I visited; it over-flowed into a surf of gameboxes, trains, erector struts, gun barrels, softballs, gloves. Metal twinkles drifted everywhere among the rest of that rich jumble like stars in a little homemade sky which opened my mind, as the machine did, but to a life I think I associated with the word Heaven then. What still disturbs me is my first clear flicker of conscience: every time he left me alone in that room of his I'd pick out a small toy I'd been coveting and pocket it or stuff it into my schoolbag. I can't remember his name. I know he knew I was stealing from him, but it must have been worth it to him just to have someone his age drop in once or twice a week. His skinny, tall, stooped-over, humble kindness, his delight at my arrivals, his calm surrender of desire or will, at his age no doubt inculcated by suffering, saves me today. My mother knew his mother and I was ordered to visit him, play with him at least once a week, be nice to him, be good. Is my childhood friend alive? What has his life been like? Does he wear one of those braces: flat shiny chrome struts jut out of the pants leg on either side of the ankle to the arch of the shoe where they meet a rod going across under the foot, like a stirrup? I can't remember anything we said, but I keep seeing that knowing sincere smile he had, whenever I'd buzz his door and he opened it. I keep seeing myself filching a yo-yo, top or pimple ball. No more than two or three. Then I abandoned him, never went back. Who wants someone who's crippled, has to stay home all day, has to be taken care of? God, what it is to be young, so young that consciousness is barely born. Back then all needs are yours; then, all you're strong enough to know is you, a you that barely exists. But I needed someone to forgive me—and he did. After all, kids know when a toy is missing, even when they have more than they need. His tenderness returns now, he leans above me like a saint, waiting, my hand searches his toys—his warm hurt eyes accept me: a gaze that says gratitude for friendship is easy, no matter what its terms, his pity and hatred hold me.

Bob came from Union City where his father and socialite mother
still lived on a dreary blue-collar street, in a narrow dark row house.
Dr. Ockene had made millions in Hollywood performing safe, illegal
abortions and lived like this now to hide it, Bob said. The first time
my plump, resentful, overdressed, hostile fate appeared in the quad
at Penn where we were Freshmen living in the same dorm, he was
wearing a J. Press tweed jacket, Brooks Bros. shirt and rep tie, Brooks
cordovan brogues, all the Ivy League trappings of a rich boy prepped
at The Hill School. His yellowish oily moonface, stubby nose and
close blue eyes, flimsy blond hair, his always clean square-cut man-
icured nails, fit perfectly my picture of privilege. His cheeks were so
full there were dimples just below the top of his cheekbones near
the eyes. He had a pot belly, too, a kind of early prosperous bloat.
For some reason he "admired" me, he said, he had a strangely
inflated view of my mind, my writing gifts, my "honesty and
innocence," at the beginning of our friendship. This was in '52, I
think, 7½ years after The Bomb, the start of a new undoing and
reseeing of morality that's still harrowing us, though it can't tran-
scend our lust for war and money. We did the usual things together:
started a literary magazine, went to a whorehouse on the campus for
one shot, visited New York a lot, dated together, drank, listened to
jazz, read and talked about books. Then I quit Penn, lived in Boston
for a year, came back to New York, went to Iowa, then Mexico for
two years then home again to Philly, where we resumed our friend-
ship. This is introductory, but I want you to know, I'm trying to
define, to understand, to accept, what happened to me about 10 years
after Bob and I met when I got back from Mexico. I was teaching
college, we had one small daughter, Millie was pregnant, we were
living on a 300 acre, mostly wooded old Philadelphia family farm
in the huge farmhouse overlooking the Schuylkill from a hill whose
mile-long stretch of grass and bushes swept down to the river and

turnpike on the other side. The living room fireplace was so big you could stand in it. One late Friday winter afternoon, Ockene arrived from New York. He was working for a publisher, and had shifted from Preppie snottiness to humble leftwing anti-Johnson anti-middleclass anti-anything-USA, had started to wear Army-Navy surplus khaki jackets and fatigues, read everything by Beckett, attended marches, edited only political books. Bob also had started to use drugs, and, as with other things, had become a connoisseur—of pot. He'd buy as many kinds as possible, pay anything for a chance to sample a new variety, would smoke daily. That day, he brought a bag of something he called "special," something dipped in something, something rare. Mexican, Turkish, I can't remember. We sat around, Bob and I, eating and drinking, smoking. Somehow I smoked maybe 7 or 8 joints, not noticing, then, just as Bob switched on the fluorescent light under the sink—it's still hard to believe— the instant the light flashed on, me watching Bob, Bob looking at me, I *was* the light, whoever I was flashed into terror, the light was me, everything was bathed in terror, no difference between my terror and what I saw—chairs, the Wedgwood blue walls and moldings, oak table piled high with turkey scraps and fruit—reason didn't work, from one click of the wall clock's second hand to the next it happened, I had "punctured the most vulnerable part of my ego," everything was outside *and* inside, my mind was the world, the world was my mind. At one point Ockene and I sat in a darkened room and I begged him for help, and he hissed at me—"Now you know what it is to be insane," "Now you know what it is to be dead," and I pleaded with him not to talk that way, to take it back. I realize now how much he hated me, but much more how he hated his own, confused, hating self. I knew he had tried to kill himself once in his bedroom at his parents' house, but the sound of his body hitting the floor woke his mother and she saved him, and it began to dawn on me—he made me him in his mind so he could kill himself, so he could die and survive, like a god, he converted me into a human sacrifice that would save him from himself. I refused to see Ockene after that. There were a few phone calls, an incident about a book of mine. On his last, unannounced visit, he brought along the local fake guru-druggie-political-visionary, Einhorn, who years later murdered his girlfriend and stashed her body in a trunk. They tried to convince me of the benefits of LSD. After that, nothing between us for five years. Then one day he called, out of the blue: we talked, and, casually, he told me he had seen his doctor after a three-month flu and was told he had Leukemia. Nothing to worry about, "treatable." Bob's voice was bland, insipidly detached, out of touch. I was shocked and told him so, but he was convinced it was nothing. A year later, he was hospitalized. Millie and I drove in to Mt. Sinai to see him. His belly was bloated like a basketball where the spleen had swelled, there was a big black magic-marker X drawn on the right side of his belly—to target the radiation. We talked. I felt nothing. No: I was glad I wasn't him. I was glad he was there. I kissed him and we left. About a year later a friend of ours told me how she stayed with him at his bedside for two days while he died, how terribly "hard" it was for him to die. At the Quaker ceremony, a shrink friend of Bob's stood up in the silence, said he loved Bob, then affectionately proposed that Bob's blood was "boiling," Bob was "always angry but never expressed it directly," "boiling . . . and that's Leukemia." Bob was a vehicle of luck that took weeks of psychosis, years of struggle, to understand, of being reborn, of trying to cope with myself as someone whose life had been plunged into panic in an eyeblink. How can I define the scar? Amazing how things happen, how Ockene was drawn to me, admired me, as he said, how a life can change, how I wanted to be close to his arrogant uppercrust pose of superiority, of absolute taste. I remember everyone looked different when I broke: my terror, their otherness, their distance from what I felt, made me feel as if I were swimming inside a mammoth tank of water, the water was between us, and outside happy benign spectators were sustained by a life I knew was forever lost to me—the daily world we love because it's safe, common, familiar. I felt I'd evaporate in an instant and not exist, ever, every moment not exist, I was without identity, a pinpoint of pure fear. Over and over I'd hear my voice grieving at this, this loss of . . . "me." I'd stand out on the slate back porch and look down the grassy hill into the distance at trees, sky, cars on the turnpike, and feel the pull of space, feel I could be sucked out like a breath—the "me" and "it" of life was a carnage of fear and disbelief—all world, all ungraspable world. All image of myself, no world. I clung to the world as if it were me, or clung to me as if I were the world. The air was desperate. I was the air. Chores or activities could distract me—eating, love-making, a movie, sweeping, making beds—anti-disasters. It took at least twenty years for that terror drop by drop to seep back into the soul of the world, where it came from, to seep back to the bottom of my soul, where it belongs. Maybe fate gave me a look at the *first* god, the one before all the ones that followed—Zeus, Christ, Aph-rodite, Ra, Hermes, Yaweh, any of the names—maybe the great gift is what comes from within that forces you to build a whole new self on nothingness, to survive—a you without you, a man with a name without a name with a face without a face until he cares about nothing except now, as these words come to me, now. I guess gods do exist. I have to confess I believe one of them, disguised as a human, visited me. "The gods have become diseases," Jung claimed, but I think not. Whatever has had the power to break us we call god. In those days, whatever was inside us we couldn't accept—that made time palpable, too slow, disastrous with the blindness of the long cleansing of a life—was what beckoned the soul to consciousness.

These days faith and salvation have put down fresh roots in our life, authority's the insatiable need for a personal vision, a peek at the ever-nagging possibility of a realm or entity that would prove a portion of us lasts, persists forever after flesh has been incinerated or digested into the earth. Not bones or teeth like you see on TV anthropology shows, not lumps and gritty ash in an urn, but some essence of the self that wept and laughed, grateful for another's face, some chance at sanctity we can't stop revising like a hopeless poem that chokes us, some crumb of I, me, you, her, us, some . . . something.

When I think of it now I still see just how ugly and dirty the place was, what a bare unprotected monk-like life it was that year, living first in the old tire warehouse on the outskirts of town, no toilet or sink, no furniture, nothing except two ratty mattresses, fruit crates, blankets from home, unfinished splintery lath walls, gobs of hard gray mortar squeezed between bricks, and everywhere the acrid stink of tire rubber, dirt and dust, everywhere in high black stacks truck tires, car tires, hundreds, except for one small room, probably an office once, where we slept and read. The teeth-like treads gleamed in the dark. Some nights I'd choke with asthma from the filth, from rage, from how far away home was. Some nights we'd lie in our room reading by the sallow light of the small bulbs of the bed lamps we got at a junk shop and nailed up on our walls. Outside the fields of Iowa went on forever, a ditch of yellow mud bordered the north wall. Some nights Bob and I would bundle up in everything we owned and go out and stare at the shoals of stars, pale surfy swarms pulsing slightly, stand half-drunk in the lampless cityless darkness rambling about poetry, family, sex, loneliness. Once, I remember, I took out an old silver Bach cornet I picked up in a pawnshop for 15 bucks and tried to play the thing, stood on the edge of the ditch leaning back, pointing the horn straight at the sky, but all that came were squawking mewing fartlike tuneless wails, jagged held notes. At one point—the horn against my lips—I took a wrong step into the ice-crusted watery slough and stumbled and fell and almost broke off my front teeth. For months I carried the mouthpiece in my pocket, fondling it, taking it out to heft, practicing on it to build my lip, *fweeting* a few raw notes whenever I felt like it— walking across campus, on the street. I kept myself company like that, I became somebody else, mostly Bix because I envied his sweet pure tone, the steadiness and range, his strict, condensed phrasing, the direct brevity of his style, a miraculously articulated, triumphant sadness. Before long we took an apartment in the heart of town—bought new mattresses, desks, two chairs, built bookcases with cinderblocks and boards—two rooms, high doors between, where we'd write, often at the same time early in the morning or late at night. It was wonderful being serious about writing, believing oneself able to hear someone hearing your voice, to hold a human gaze, wonderful feeling haunted, if you were lucky, by lines, impulses, hot formless combinations of phrases that led your hands over the keys at a speed beyond understanding, beyond experience. Then out would come the paper with words on it and you'd begin again—chop, change, shift, hack, put something back or stick it somewhere else, anything seemed possible in that mood—to hear the necessary mind of the poem. Otherwise it was classes and the usual college shit: football games, parties, gossip, worry about grades. Then the snow came and everything was lost under it, everything slowed. Sometimes it fell neck-deep. People wallowing through would shovel paths on the sidewalks. You'd see heads floating along the top of the snow walls. The quads and fields were cratered and scarred with ruts like a moon map glowing blue-white. Hard to describe the mood of Iowa City after one of those big snows, but I was happier than I knew then, trapped there, purified of choice by isolation, schedules breaking down, the roads out of town impassable. We'd stay up till three or four in the morning, playing pinball machines in an all-night diner a few blocks away, or reading, trying to write. The vividness of words on a page in a book, the sound of the human on a printed page, was never more compelling and intense than on those long nights of immense calm while the snow under the street lamps lay there, consolingly white and quiet, going on for miles. The Workshop quonsets looked like sleeping animals, down by the Iowa River. You could walk across it and not break through; you could see the wide brown road of water underneath roiling past. The uncountable rows of footprints crossing and recrossing, the snowy lid of ice, made my scalp prickle. It looked eerie, too meaningful—why, I still can't figure out—that bright, pocked, luminous crust scored by those shadowy holes. And nothing came there, not at night in the bleak Midwestern cold, unless an animal happened by. At night if you drove out of town (after the roads were plowed, snow mounded ten feet high on either side), where it seems nothing exists but fields, endless open fields, if you looked across the glowing sugary land, you might say that the silence and peace you were at one with had always been and always would be.

Isolated, old, face down, Reds is stretched across his bed on the
second floor, wheezing, terrified, mumbling to Charlie about death,
so drained by flu and asthma he can't even jack himself up an inch
on his arms. I go downstairs. Wood's everywhere—shelves, kitchen
utensils, pegs, notched sticks to prop up ropes, chairs, boxes. A glow
bleeds from everything, like spirit, swept clean, mysteriously lovely,
some deep irrational force ordering it the way coastlines and rocks
simply are, and are beautiful. The two-storey suburban house set
hundreds of feet back from the street is eggshell white inside except
for the stripped walnut moulding on windows and doors, the floor,
a few raw Oriental rugs. There's also, I start to notice, biking gear
hung on pegs—black skin-tight shorts that stop at the knee, black
cleated perforated leather shoes without heels, a gauzy tutti frutti
cap, "Cinelli" stamped on the peak. A few years ago his asthma
almost killed him; allergic to himself, he could barely breathe. I
visited him in the hospital; steroids dripped into his arm. Day after
day talking with him, watching, some hours in silence, I'd wait for
the words I thought he needed, I needed. None. Then slowly he came
back, but not completely, ever. Some circulatory thing had killed
nerves in toes and fingertips so now he bikes like mad to stay alive
at least 16 miles twice daily around "The Loop" on the Schuylkill
River past the Art Museum, past rock hillsides and cherry trees,
rowers, sunbathers, statues, long green banks. To build his lungs and
legs, his wind, to survive. Master Carpenter Reds had done finish
work for big law offices and such in Philly, but this house is purely
for himself, Reds has put it together out of his lonely mind. No
women; nothing; nothing but this. Charlie is still upstairs, I can hear
the hum of his talking. A tool chest, 3' x 3' x 3', unvarnished sanded
elm, lapped edges deliberately left raw, black iron pins holding it
together, is pushed against a wall. Beside it's a short, wide ladder,
too delicate to stand on, three whimsical rungs, an "idea ladder"

draped with gloves, wet socks, shirts, useless except to dry belongings on. The light: luminous haze as in a chapel. Now I tip toe back upstairs and stand outside the bedroom door and hear Charlie, sitting with his back to me, talking. Facing away from Charlie, on his belly, Reds has on Wigwam rag socks, his feet point down over the bedside, his grayish red-flecked beard stubbles his cheeks and chin. I step back and slip into the garret a few feet away: three bike rims O O O on pegs on a white wall, and a length of clothesline running, sagging from the window frame on the far wall to the door. Dishrags, a biking shirt and socks, touch in a cluster. A rim is locked in a wooden workshop vise; tools laid out in a row. A bike frame, periwinkle blue, floats out on two fine wires from the ceiling, an icon, the key to a lost religion. Everything in this place seems sacred, burnished with wax and oil, everything's needed, everything comes from one source. I rest my hand on the cool aluminum hoop in the vise. Snow veils the grass, a dour scruffy brightness. All this time, over an hour, the light hasn't changed. I imagine it never changes here. I pick up a pair of pliers from the bench and squeeze the handles hard and feel the little give they have and let go. For a time I believe this aura I am in is a peace I must hold forever at the heart of my life, but it withers. I stand still, quieted by what I have entered. Bits of difficult breathing drift into the room. Hacking. Rags of talk. A scooped-out gray lightness like not being here or anywhere, and, off and on, something unbearable, a glimpse of another human hell I'm afraid might never stop, will increase, will trap me—like being, always, here, like him, like this. Nobody else has a house like this. Nothing else is like this, this trio, us. I ease past their two figures— one hunched forward over the other, in bed, prostrate, facing away—and go downstairs. Hopelessness seeps out of the wood and cleanly plastered walls, an inexplicable comfort. On the lawn a dark something darts by. Not one sound. The world, a disappearance, this house, these last things one man wants, are. No wonder God keeps pounding at our brains, awake, asleep, no wonder the misery of His silence is so much a part of who we are we do not recognize it. No wonder Reds used black iron nails to make that box for his tools, each countersunk, unfilled, so the rough heads would show. From where I sit, across the room, they look like Something's eyes. No movement anywhere. An abyss. That's it. The surfaces, the shapes, the patience and the care, nails tapped in perfectly, the distances between them poignant, smooth surfaces, howling knots. . . . Nothing need move. Ever. The bicycle upstairs, no seat, no handlebars or wheels, is truth suspended in air, its bare bright forktips will never touch the floor. Each breath a terrible price. Charlie's coming downstairs. I have to stop this.

A man standing in the half-moon park across from The Franklin Institute is bent over studying his white skinny leg, the right leg, his pants leg's rolled to the middle of his thigh, which looks as thin as his calf. Summer is over. Brown claw-like leaves fill the gutters, litter pavements and grass. Whiffs of decay and letting-go, pungent, sweet, an exhilarated sinuous ease. I stroll by along the curved trimmed edge of the grass, stop and watch him run his hands over the leg, searching its muscles, squeezing his knee cap, kneading, probing. The long critical tendons behind the knee are vivid as he swings his leg to test it. He doesn't wear those grit-glazed rags that hang as if they're soaked, waxy with time and sweat, his cuffs aren't shreds that drag the ground, no fly's askew or gaping. The usual stretch of belly, that looks like dirt has been rubbed into the skin for make-up to prepare a character—Poverty, say—in a medieval passion play, isn't there. The man looks baffled. A pale fish-blue glow hovers on his skin, the thigh especially, while he still scrutinizes each inch of flesh. Now his upside-down face just about touches the front of his thigh, like a child straining to learn new words. Eyes. Hands. What passion we have for ourselves. Poor us, poor Bill today with his heart attack, poor Warren with leukemia, poor everyone. What passion? Those smooth, cool egg-shaped rocks strewing the Cape Ann beaches are what I want, near-perfect spheres, pitted, grayish tan granite voids jostled together by the sea in a consolation of eons. When I was there last week, I lurched digging my heels maybe 25 feet down the sand cliffside behind the house onto the beach three late afternoons in a row and tottered among rocks—sky deepening pink—looking for ones I wanted to keep near me. You have to stoop as close as you can, stepping, looking, you have to seize intuitively— that one!—or you won't find those that are just for you. It took hauling the six I picked one at a time up the cliff by thrusting each into the steep sand every few feet to keep from slipping back, cradling it up up up to the ledge at the top where they stayed until I lugged them back to our rented house overlooking the Atlantic. A lighthouse like a hydrant sits on a spit of land out there. At night it moans. I also stuffed several stones into my pockets—for their colors, for their heft and feel, creases, streaks, for a spray of dots, lichen rosettes, dents, textures, messages. One, if you hold it up to the sky in daylight, lets light through, goes milky inside and glows. The big rocks are out back now on the edge of our garden at home huddled in a loose pile I see mornings over coffee. They will never vanish under waves again. I love how delicately they touch. But the miracle is their blindness, those blind blind silent things. Blind to the world and to themselves.

The entire hood and top and trunk of the white 1950s 4-door Cadillac
sedan was covered with bird cages, bird houses, each one slightly
different, each one lovingly fitted and painted stick by stick, slat by
slat, by the fat, smiling, legless man sitting near his car on the side
of the road that summer day about noon. Pinewoods followed the
road for miles. We were driving to the beach when we saw him,
wheelchair and all, smoking a cigarette in the shimmering heat,
sweating, tipping his Phillies cap as we pulled up, so jovially
ensconced, the look on his face so secure that it delighted us to stop,
get out, admire his handiwork and ask how he did it and what had
happened to his legs. The stumps began above where his knees had
been. They barely reached the edge of the heavy nylon seat. Viet-
nam, a land mine, the details reported as casually as you'd tell a
friend about your trip to Jamaica. There was post-vacation euphoria
in his tone, and not a shred of self-pity, nothing weighty or grave,
nothing to induce sympathy, only gratitude for being alive, happi-
ness at having become "the best bird cage and bird house maker on
the entire east coast." Anything that came up he enjoyed, anything
sad or tragic he'd make beautiful, instructive, necessary. It was as if
some law of fate had been revealed to him, as if he had seen the
wisdom, of "Faith is the knowledge that Destiny is Providence," and
lived it, could always find some grain of sweetness even in the
meanest event, then identify it to help you love. I patted his head as
if he were a child, just for a second though, surprised I had done it.
At one point he reached through the back window of his car and
fished out a local tabloid, snapped it open to pages 3 and 4 where a
two-page spread on his war experiences and recovery and his flour-
ishing business showed him with legs, back then: before the war,
posing in front of his barracks; and now: just as he was, selling his
wares on the road, the hot chaotic south Jersey pines hissing and
thrashing behind him. There were also shots of him at home at his

workbench, sawing dowels for the cages, cutting up short slats for the houses, coping a special burst of filigree or carving a decorative relief, "depending on his mood," the story said. Amazing, his lack of pride, the pleasure he got from ordinary talk, his immediate friendliness, the matter-of-fact way he took me through the article in the paper, how glad he looked standing at attention in his uniform the year he enlisted, then his joy on the day he received his electric stainless steel wheelchair, the rims of its thick fat rubber tires gleaming. Just below the armrests his hands drooped on the white-walled tires. In all shots he was smiling: his eyes said, "Christ, good to see you, whoever you are, good to be here!" I know a man, Dan Gottlieb, friend of a friend of mine, who smiled like that even after his car went out of control and crashed one night when a truck tire flew off its axle from the opposite side of the highway and smashed through his windshield. The night after the accident, Jeff and I sped to his hospital in Reading. He was in full body traction. Part of the rig was a triangular brace held by three screws (the top half of their shafts stuck out) driven into his shaved skull—top, and each side— to immobilize his head. The damage to his spine was so severe he would never walk again. He could still move lips, eyes and arms, and a few fingers, a little. We stood there talking. Suddenly one of us started joking about sex, foreplay especially, about how you'd better be able to keep it going forever, use your tongue, etc., you know, the macho shit men revel in because it magnifies everything so they can detach and feel for a few glorious moments like sexual giants. I remember telling the "iron tongue" joke, which elicited Dan's feeble laugh. Soon we subsided, soon it was time for him to sleep. Before his eyes closed one last time that night he looked at each of us, smiled, and said, in a dull flat distant shell of a voice, muffled by drugs, "God, I'm glad you're here!" The hospital room glistened with equipment, its atmosphere of emergency a strange relief from the boredom of routine in our lives, one sweet young nurse tending the floor, on a shelf above his head Dan's heart on the monitor screen a jumpy blue trace.

Jesus, how many of these people haunt the street? Nine at night and this one starts doing a jig with a ghost, hugs someone only he can see, then as if he's caught me spying on him, stops dancing, stands stock still, lets his arms hang limp, stares straight at me perched on the barstool in the waist-high picture window, then begins another, crazier dance—call it "the killer tango," the familiar get-rid-of-it-all-I-can't-stand-it dance that heals our disappointed hearts, our at-least-once-ruined forever-smashed hearts. He presses a rifle butt against his shoulder, leans his cheek down behind the hammer, sights, points at my head. I've decided not to take my eyes off this nut, his technique is so convincing, his ability to use The Invisible so deft. He lives in the world he sees inside himself: he's a terrific natural actor. Now he's lecturing a crowd—on war, on why we've turned him into a penniless psychotic doomed to the streets—his lips curl, chew and spit out words, he keeps jabbing his finger into someone, into something—accusatory snarls—shifts his feet like a boxer, feints, ducks, throws a flurry of punches, his arms shoot up like flares, he stiffens and holds them there in a Nixon V, the bare black O of his mouth and bright bug eyes flash with harsh embryonic vapor-arc blue. A drink jangles behind me. Ripples of talk. Piano. He lifts a phantom hunting bow, fits an unreal arrow to an impalpable string, draws it back until it dents his cheek, freezes, aims, relaxes, lets go, the shaft passes through my chest so fast it's nothing, as innocuous as not being able to hear his mouthings at the glass.

A young guy, homosexual, I guess, steps into a decorator's wall-to-wall carpeted store window across the street and stands among mirrors, lounge chairs, lamps, tasseled silk cushions, overblown *dreck* people who don't know what they really like buy. Hands splayed on his hips, he rolls his hips, slowly, over and over. Tight tan jeans, pink see-through shirt, a wrangler's hat the color of his pants, tilted back so I can see the pasty aloof bland face that looks like a dummy's—you know, you'll be shopping in a department store and glimpse one of those flesh-colored presences beside you and feel it's human but know it's not but feel it is, in other words for a moment not know who or what it is. I'm sitting in an orthopaedic surgeon's office, waiting to have tape taken off my arm and shoulder, reading a magazine, and when I look up he's in the window, performing his lewd pelvic drawl, oblivious of the world beyond the black lacquered tables, glass shelves and shots of movie stars. I'm not sure just how long I've been watching when he freezes, stops circling his hips, plants his feet about three feet apart on a red rug, fixes his hands on his hips, and stares at me. Tapered polished nails. Cock-bulge. Zombie face. His eyes grow clearer, larger, as I gaze, doze, then jerk awake, dreaming he has stepped through the window to join me. Alone, we're so alone, I think, as I look over at the people in the room, reading, napping, chatting, waiting in their chairs. Nobody's in the window now, but his lust and slick intimacy's in the air, in me. I glance over to see whether he has stepped back into shadow to take a break behind the wild-flowered chintz sofa. Not one person on the street has stopped to consider him in there. Twin bent-back gilded Egyptian hands pedestalled for book ends; between them, three or four leather-bound classics, spines stamped gold. Lana Turner and Glenn Ford framed in oval silver. A crystal vase crowded with silk flowers. Sun blazes on the rug, the window's a haze tinted crimson—in a recent nightmare, the same nebulous blood shade on all the buildings; torpedoes menacing a hundred Philadelphia streets. My name. The nurse calls my name.

Both wear dark blue hairline pin stripe suits, Old Spice cologne, mirror-bright black wing tips, styled wet haircuts—rushing in front of me on the corner to cross the street, so lost in talk I miss their faces, so vile with worry all I hear is the wake of their agitated voices—". . . and I thought that in 1978, after striving so . . . just to keep my head above water . . ." The stateliness of "striving" disgusts me. I pick out a winesap from a stand, pay, stuff it in my pocket, intrigued by the puzzle of his words, of his misery-ridden tirade. The sun's steady and full, almost warm: early October; grapes, pears, limes, oranges, burnished, innocently gay. Morning. 1992 now. I stop at Rindelaub's for coffee, toasted bagel, unfold my *New York Times* on the sticky rag-streaked counter, skim story after story. The waitress clears my plate, asks if I want more coffee. Half a cup. A girl on my right snaps down a tip under her saucer and leaves. The bakery section bustles with housewives intent on breads and cakes. A vestige of cheap cologne. The pained tone of his voice ". . . just to keep my head above water . . . " pleads, descends, echoes, dissolves. I feel either I forgot to do something very important and will be punished, or shame has trickled back from an old source I can't identify: "'I know' does not tolerate a metaphysical emphasis." Another way to say it is—who I am and where I am are two parts of a puzzle whose other pieces are lost, and I grieve for every missing piece. Everyone's gone. The red leatherette stool tops look silly empty; each one's wavy, shiny, stretched from the weight of custom-ers. I wipe crumbs to the floor, get up, hand the cashier my check with the right money and push open the door. Out on the street, ". . . and I thought that in 1978, after striving so hard just to keep my head above water, clear. . ." Perched on velvet pedestals in a store window a few doors down—wallets, purses—their elegant glossy skins, their darknesses, their thin mute lips.

Stitches have popped and unravel, the coat collar of the woman sitting beneath me on the aisle is coming apart, her shoulder bumps my thigh, her dense black rag of a wig is spray-sheened, each earring a tin snake hoop swallowing its tail, the spotty fake gold-dip plating, once buffed bright to help them sell, all but gone now. Her face is a blank. My face—I can feel the moral part of me choosing it—has a smile on, a forced poise in this atmosphere of poor and black and What can be done? What can *I* do? I don't look hard at anyone, I don't hate, I don't want to be on a bus whose heat works, or is clean; I follow the buildings as we pass, inhaling Woolworth perfume, mothballs, musty wool. Frost sweats on the window corners. A kid at the back hunches over, cups his hands between his legs. Sweet whiffs of grass. We careen by the Museum of Natural History, tipped into each other, standing, seated, scowling because we touch. The humped, tapering dinosaur profile fills the Museum's front window, as always, its back fins wide gray spikes of shadow. When I got home today a police car was nosed up onto the sidewalk, Millie and Margot were getting out. A cop was helping. Someone on the 33 had tried to tear my father's gold watch off Millie's wrist, he kept trying to pull it off, jamming his fingers under the strap in front of everyone, as if the bus were empty. He wanted what he saw and couldn't break the strap and Millie had to identify him at the precinct, file a complaint, then testify. Last night I heard her say, for the first time since I've known her, "I'm afraid, hold me." A whisper, a childlike, low cry. "I woke up, seeing the man again . . . on the bus." One of my writing students handed out copies of a poem in which a friend's mother is dying of cancer, she's sitting on the bed with her daughter, who holds her hand, and—the woman stops breathing and as she dies she screams and a block away, the neighbors, hearing it, ends the poem. Listen. Sometimes a kind of psalm—parable without an

ending, no point, no moral, nothing to use or live by—is what I hear,
its rending unidentifiable brute tone, its plot of helpless non-human
eyes meaning God knows what.

"Be a Christian!" she screams, but instead I open my fly, pull out my shlong, chase her through the house and she flings open the door, runs into the street laughing, runs back inside. We'd been bickering in the kitchen—about money, kids, cocksucking, swallowing cum, defining pleasure and obligation, disease and meaning, all the stuff that comes up in a thirty-year-old marriage, and I insist that getting one's cock sucked is essential, I will not be swayed, I become the King of Chaos & Doubt, demanding satisfaction, using my cowardice as a sword, refusing to agree, being a complete rat, laughing at morality, I just stand there leering like a moron, refusing to be moved, her telling me to look in the mirror at my three-day beard and dirty hair, turn myself over to the local church for the homeless, me leaning against shelves of pots and pans, her wagging a silly righteous finger at me. It's true, I have no religion. I'm no Christian, no Jew. God's outside the power of my hand or mind. I can't change the thin gold afternoon haze that makes the yard look peaceful. But I've given to the poor, kissed dogs, been forced to the wall of prayer, crouched inside doubts like black cocoons, and seen only one true way: the people I love—may the earth's blessing of acceptance reach their ears.

I walk in unzipping my fly, enter a stall, let my pants drop, sit on the cool black plastic horseshoe-shaped toilet seat, pants at my ankles, elbows on knees, head down, and leave the green steel door open when this guy, about sixty, comes in and I look up just as he pops out his dick to piss in one of the urinals, glancing back at me over his shoulder. I think my bare crotch must offend him the way his eyes skid over me. I think he thinks, "Why doesn't that creep close his door?" so I jerk my knees out of the way, swing it around, blank gray, flip up the chrome latch tongue into its keeper and hear—"You were probably too young to remember but seeing you like that reminded me of what it was like in the Ford plant in Chester in the early 30s—unions, you know, people don't understand why they exist—they had rows of toilets and Ford ordered all the doors taken off so you could see if the man in the stall was really taking a shit or just goofing off. At the head of each row they stationed some jerkoff to watch and clock in and out every single worker from the second his ass hit the seat to the second he left the stall." In front of me, my blank door. His shoes scraping the stone floor, the pneumatic men's room door closing *wsss wsss wsss*.

In Provincetown last month I wandered into a shop where they sell carved birds, decoys, decorative gulls, prefabricated unpainted ducks and whittled local birds, fifty or so different sizes and colors. In one corner on the edge of an old marble mantle a faded shore bird, less legs and pedestal, lay on its side. I picked it up and held it. Light blue feathery strokes had been flicked all over the darker shade of its modest pear of a body by "Willard," its dead maker. Its head was the size of a fat, burnished grape, its three-inch beak the snapped-off end of a wooden knitting needle. Nostrils had been picked into the side of the dowel, tiny dark hollows. Its silent life had started in the thirties, according to the date on its belly. Scratches next to the signature. It had been stuck on somebody's front lawn for years to attract its kind, the salesman said. Its eyes were casual gouges, dull holes with nothing in them, sockets, done with a knife point, not those two-tone tacked-on shoe buttons that gleam and seem to stare. In life, it lets out one of the few precise cries interpreting existence—harsh, isolate, storyless, unadorned, like scrap metal shearings scraped against each other in brief tentative clarity. You could try all your life to make that sound come out of you when you felt it and you'd fail. I put down twenty bucks and still have seventy left to pay before they mail it to me and I can see it again. Right now it's Sunday, chilly early fall. A door, a bus, feet, street voices, pierce the windows—". . . no, no, I can't . . . " ". . . but if you'd only . . . try . . . just try" as if from a mindless throat's—whose?—pointless agony.

Whenever I open the *Diaries* I feel he knows each sick quirk of mine
from all sides, down to the root. Last night in my studio I stayed up
late. Both volumes, *1910-1913*, *1914-1923*, lay on my desk, face up.
"I feel restless and vicious." he writes in those pages. Almost every
night he etched his mind on paper: analyzing, describing dreams,
scenes from the day, obsessed with knowing why, morality gnawing
his skull like a rat. Moonlight gave the slick blackish-blue covers a
luminous, angelic sheen—shot from above, fifteen tiny pedestrians
amble across the famed stone bridge in Prague: statues of beasts and
heroes, water smooth and blue. His furred, elfin wedge of a face in
the famous portrait seemed to cleave the air. Purgatorial glee strode
from his eyes, I thought, salvation always at his fingertips, always
light-years away. O gentle Jewish mirror, so much worse off than
anyone, you mastered the saintly art of doubt. Paralyzed, transcen-
dent, always at the point of departure, each moment conscious of
"the truth of the vanishing moment," you "trace pain on the left
side" of your head and predict you won't reach forty because of your
"inner leprosy," the word "once," you sigh, "explodes that darkness
on which memory draws." February 13: "The possibility of serving
with all one's heart." What can it mean? To caress infinity? To see
God's face dominate the sky?

An image sketched in a void, delicate pencil lines forming a street: a man flat on his back, arms out, head lolled over, a mutt sniffing the man's neck under his chin, some witnesses. Above the faceless face, lapsed away from the spectators, a shape persists like the breath of a miscreated god, like a burst of exhaust in cold, a ghostly residue belonging to a different, finished story that hovers near you the way thought does when it occurs as a phrase that explains something unseen connected to something known then fades to a sliver of memory. Once in a dream I saw my life take shape, a story whose entire meaning is easily understood—who, what, where, why, when—about real people and things, essential to the world, and when I woke everything—sheets, blankets, rugs, chairs, walls, shoes—were radiant like men in myths who killed and drank hard and hated death and were consumed by envy of the Gods because they existed and infused humans with their impossible immortal glory.

Like fierce ice some voice keeps wailing, like a wall it's always there, and I don't even know whether it comes from inside or rises out of the streets or winter stubble fields nearby, from car lots, from the sky, but it keeps coming. I was reading Stone's *A Flag For Sunrise*, the TV had on one of its numb redundant soaps, it flickered just beyond the page tops as I read about the hippie girl's body jacknifed beneath frozen vegetables and meat in the Lieutenant's food freezer in South America and the priest orders him to lift it out and dump it, and it seemed fierce ice was everywhere, as a human sound, it seemed waking and dreaming were the same. This happened to me only once before, after a drug panic: I could touch and taste and hold, but it was like slipping through to the nether side of time where things have not yet been, but are about to be born and pass through us here so quickly they're impossible to see. I'd stand in front of my hi fi speakers and the temperatures of brass, strings, tympani would sear or freeze me; I'd lie down, listen, hesitate, slide out of myself like surf retreating. If God existed and could receive us, speak and forgive, would it matter? Who can undo what we are? Like an assault—dark street, late, footsteps, something behind you—the world can become fierce ice, no voice, face, or meaning, and you will have to walk through it, seeking the ghost of someone you have loved too much, and can never have. Stripped of flesh and bone, presence without location, misery without a name, how do we survive the dread warps of identity? I was reading, and the priest brushed away ice dust from the wrapped foods and reached in and felt the red-haired innocent skull of a girl.

Poco allegro, allegro con brio the oldsters sit in the classroom, waiting for Dvorak's 8th and 10th, on a rainy April day. There they are, gabbing, waiting for the music, for the black plastic arm to ascend then halt then float down gently onto the record. The professor stands in front of the class, organizing notes, fussing with a book on the lectern. I've passed this room before: first music, then a lecture, then the students rambling on about the beauty of the notes, about what this passage and that movement mean. This tender little group of white-haired people, listening together, warms me like a woman who listens while I confess pain or love and then, as unassumingly as sunlight increases to brighten flowers on the table where I sit, takes my hand in her hand. I'm standing behind them at the door, amplifier on a shelf under the green chalkboard, two brown shelf speakers flanking the desk, silver turntable spinning as the arm descends and the teacher looks up, *poco allegro, allegro con brio* chalked in shaky tall white letters on the board. The needle catches, static before music. Tilting their heads back, up straight, elbows on knees, heads down, eyes open, closed, not hearing themselves, not seeing themselves, hoping to be overwhelmed, backs to me, they sit.

There is this woman in the street screaming, "Take it away, take it out of my head . . ." long red socks crumpled at her ankles, fat blotchy legs, filthy raincoat and face and hair, and everywhere on earth starvation, murder, the stark ruins of lives. But what about children, beautiful, loveable children, what about my good job and compassion and the fifty cents I gave without hesitation to the brain damaged, drunk whatever-he-was, crumbs of his last bite spit-gleaming on his lips, what about memories of love? She paces the same spot. Everything is politics, and nothing is; everything is the family; everything is delicacy, detail, perception. No. There's only her voice, inside me and outside, in the street, and nobody can take away the way she pleads, nobody can reach in and take it out of her head. The pear tree in my yard has white blossoms everywhere, bright puffs of mist, each cupped by three of four leaves; the sky is clear blue, the clouds clear too, bustling past, wild as that voice; which reminds me of the peacock, how it loves its own beauty, utterly, until, supposedly, it catches sight of its ugly brown claws and shrieks in the agony of revelation, which makes it sound almost as poignant as one's own child screaming in pain. Words everywhere, useless desolate words. "A marvelous stillness pervaded the world, and the stars, together with the serenity of their rays, seemed to shed upon the earth the assurance of everlasting security . . . the propeller turned without a check, as though its beat had been part of the scheme of a safe universe . . . the young moon recurved, and shining low in the west, was like a slender shaving thrown up from a bar of gold . . ." That's how we want the world to be, but the woman goes on, inside, outside, and the street lets her, and the store windows show her groping by, then she's gone, then she's back in them. Everywhere the pavements are stained with old tar and car oil, everyone seems bent on accomplishing errands, the weather's mild, eerie, a bleakness spoils the edges of brightness, like the first points of rust on galvanized tin. From where I sit in my third floor study I can see it all. Once, years ago, when I was asleep, my three-year-old daughter, Margot, stood by my bed, talking to wake me, her face an inch from my face. I could feel her breath. Dawn's first light whitening. Still not really awake. Her sweet warmth. Her babbling. I woke and saw her, her head level with mine, and realized she would die. She would die one day. Nothing I could do. Her eyes. Her bright brown hair. Her clear pale skin. Little blue ducks rode little pink waves on her pajamas.

Somebody has draped a thin blue cotton jacket on a crowbar planted
in the ground across from the Franklin Institute, maybe it was set
up by one of the drunken bums who populate the benches placed
along the grassy triangle with its few old elms and oaks, its monu-
ment to local black flyers lost in WW II. The day's dense with
humidity and heat, blank threatening sky, you can taste the pollu-
tion this early as the last cars roaring in to work race each other for
the squeeze at the turn by the Museum of Natural History below me
on Logan Square. A man in a T shirt with a stick spears pieces of
paper, cups, leaves, bagging them, about a hundred feet away from
the gaunt totem—maybe it's his, which limits the mystery but
doesn't explain it. What is it? Why is it there? A coat. An iron bar,
stuck in green grass. The obvious answer's "a body," it looks like a
symbol for a body; or for when we dissolve in a moment of emptiness,
forgetfulness, and life seems to accomplish itself simply by being.
Or someone is convinced that rag on an armature is the one way he
can make clear, publicly, how he feels about himself, in the great
world, so he stuck it there, at random, in a public park. God, we're
so ordinary. We work, eat lunch, take the bus home or walk, eat
dinner, kiss, sleep, need our ambivalent baseless faith, try to "love
what is," as a dear friend put it in a letter recently. So much is silence
or privacy, and "emptiness" isn't the grace I've mentioned, but a
distance—calm for some, for others craving, dread, or the bitterness
of self-denial—a hole that grows, inside and out, real, unreal, a
continual gnawing, as if, wherever you are, whenever you can't
distract yourself, an unseen rat—call it a rat—chews on the space
beneath your heart.

One Sunday I took a bus to Pittsburgh, just for the ride. Stretched out in the aisle seat next to a well-dressed, quiet man, I started talking to him—about the weather, scenery, news. Then, in front of me, I saw the ear—the stiff miracle of its rim arcing and glowing, the fuzz of minuscule hairs, the stepped drop from the outer edge into the vestibule before the hole, the *meatus*, and then inside the skinny tunnel leading to the membrane, the chain of three small bones—*malleus, incus, stapes*—three semicircular canals, the nerve that makes sound possible. And the lobe. The wrinkles on the lobe triggered it, and some I could see on the rim, or *pinna*. Mid-afternoon sun tinted it orange, pink, red, gave it a sacred aura, made it shine. The wrinkles gripped me. They were like fine veins on a leaf, but far more delicate, deeper—it amazed me an ear could be wrinkled. The whole universe was in it, for me to decipher. I studied the ear, thinking: it welcomes the human voice, the vocalized soul, it hears anything—plaster trickling inside a wall, roofs creaking, mice, distant anonymous hammers, water, grass. The ear grew numinous in the speeding bus. Suddenly the ear was Death, the ear was a sign of Death's inescapable presence everywhere, always, and, faced with it, our awe that anything exists. I can't remember what I said, but I know I started lecturing at the man beside me, for at least fifteen minutes I sermonized on death and the ear and how we refuse to see Death in front of us, now, as it always is, in each ordinary thing, like that ear. He glanced at me, sadly, kindly, not turning his face toward me more than an inch or two, as I sang my incorrigible crazed hymn to The Death Ear. There's a faint image of him, helplessly listening, and his wary gaze, someone I never got to know. He said he was a doctor. He listened, nodded his head at times, smiled a little, me ranting about death molded out of cartilage, blood and changing light. There was snow everywhere that time of year, gulleys, hill-sides and banks splashed with it, its mushy porous streaks and rotted clumps thawing, shaped like clouds. Forty years gone. I pick up the cold key on my desk, go and slip it into the back door lock, turn it, push open the storm door, enter the night. Earth. Whisperings. Birch buds tiny as grains of rice.

So difficult to simply make a living, live, grow, take stock and slowly die, swallow life's tragic beauty, our life, so hard to accept each moment just as it is, nothing to regret, nothing better, no haunting yearned-for past, nothing but who we are *as* we are, others as they are, here, now, this insatiable web of us-and-it, instant by instant, enough. Two old dreams started this: in one I'm condemned to a retarded colony, they act numb and dopey, but powerful, like tall chunks of lead, I can't escape, even when I make my one-phone-call-a-day it's intercepted and stopped by a vague female attendant sitting at a desk in the lobby of the administration building, my universe is this long baby-blue bed-lined ward of incompetents, their tics and grunts, their blanked-out latent features, their skewed puberty of awkwardness my fixed fate. The other dream, next night, simplified to a few facts, is much more killing than the first: two male legs in trousers, brown wool trousers, dangling from the top of the frame of the dream, swaying: I stand to the left beneath them, glancing up and back, up and back, at the scuffed black work shoes on the swinging feet that twitch: soul-misery wind like wolves wailing crosses the barren scene and fills it, stays, then changes until it's insane, inclusive, pure significance, and I'm a receptor, a mere thing that hears, a "me" without identity or shape—I am the scene: torsoless legs, brown wool, black leather, background of colorless air, but mostly, now, that howl harrowing the me-world so all's the same tone of a soul that wasn't, isn't, won't be, now, but remembers itself, battling to be, the way some real person you once loved much too completely, and failed to keep, whose murderous loss lurks always near the surface, now, now, will always touch you: you hear yourself warning yourself—no avail—grief-shame's mirror suddenly held up inside you so you see the one soul you both were, still are. In waking life the punishment is clear: every night, at about three, you bolt awake.

We're seeing a shrink, I'm telling an old dream of mine: in my nursery school there's a door to the playroom, a wooden swinging door with a glass slot at eye level, and I look up from the floor where I'm playing and catch my mother's eyes inspecting me through the slot. "Voyeur," the shrink says, "your mother was a voyeur." Meaning, if you take the word literally, she got sexual pleasure from watching me, she didn't have normal sex with my father, what she loved was running her eyes over me, fondling me with her eyes as I played, absorbing me. "You wanted to put your mother's eyes out!" Emphatic, nearly elated by the "insight" she's had. And then, "You're afraid I'll swallow you." In the hall, minutes before the session, patients walked past, drugged, depressed, or terrified, slumped over mostly, slow, mumbling, gripped by some unassailable, sincere, silent chaos, and I thought, "Why don't you stand up straight, talk so I can hear you? Look at me!" the way a parent might. It was the fear of being one of them that made me want to command and punish and escape the wreck of being one of them, of having to fuse a lost child with a half-lost man now, of having to re-see others and me, of feeling that such change would take a lifetime. In most snapshots before I'm six, I'm either scowling or smiling timidly, but in a few I look away at nothing, furious at some inaccessible, unforgivable wound, and it doesn't matter who did it to me or how it happened, because only I or fate or God can heal it now. Three people: me, my wife, the female therapist, sitting close in her office decorated with houseplants, books, knickknacks, a sign taped on the file cabinet: *Be!* In one corner of a fish tank chains of bubbles gurgle up from the tip of a plastic tube. Tropicals glide, hesitate, nibble the filmy surface, wriggle up and down, browsing the glass, nosing the sandy floor for morsels of food. My wife stays quiet. Splinters of talk. Something wordless churns inside me when I ponder those eyes in the glass slot, some threat from inside me that can be almost anything but I can't find terms to believe which could formulate what it is, open and change me. A recent dream in which I strike matches again and again, trying to light a burner on our stove, letting the gas flow until the kitchen blows up and I'm pitched across the house and wake, my head echoing, erupts into words. The session's over. We get up, and smile, as always, and leave through the yawning marble hospital lobby, built for the Main Line rich, attendants, patients, doctors, visitors, indistinguishable, coming and going as we push through double doors and stop at the curb. Galvanized March glare scours the air. Plantings border the circular freshly laid black asphalt driveway and parking lot: bushes, bouquets of spiny branches, hallucinatory spring-green grass carpeted in squares: squinting, arms down, stiffened against vague danger, staring straight ahead, not touching, not speaking, not daring to seek each other's eyes—us.

In this cramped, rickety, Greenwich Village toy store, its deliber-
ately unfinished, pale, scraped wood walls and floors flecked with
streaks and clots of layered white paint, big people like us are
lumbering, stopping to peer at shelves of midget pine trees, houses,
animals, pirouetting to miss a delicate table massed with handmade,
wood Swiss haycarts, chapels, and one complete hamlet perched on
the edge of a wooden lake favored by clumps of birch. Even a few
blackbirds, trembling, frozen in air, pass over, fixed on the tips of
wires thin as hair. We look and finally buy a cute pink rabbit in a
racing car, number 9, his ears flared back by the wind, his arms
stretched out to the wheel, his hand-painted head expressively
eager, smiling into the distance in the always-present always-invis-
ible race he's in. We're at least 50 and our kids are gone, but we buy
it. For ourselves? Once we're home and unpacked we can't decide
where to put it so we leave it here, there, move it around, until, one
morning, making coffee, I see it on the counter next to my cup and
start flicking its wheels with my forefinger, crashing it, putting on
my half-glasses to inspect the endearing detail of the thumb-shaped
baby blue chassis, the creature's painted-on goggles, the fine brown
ridges brushed along the inside of his long ears. And then I see the
neck, how fragile it is, how thin the dowel of wood is that connects
his head to his skinny torso, and I have to test it. It snaps off. I snap
it off. It takes much less pressure than I thought. For a day at least
on the dining room table they lay, head next to car, a headless driver
in a race with nobody. I go by the table and look at them and don't
care, go by and wonder, go by and have thoughts, none of which I
remember, go by and rearrange the head and the car—head near
front right wheel, head three inches away from side, head touching
bumper—the driver still inside, and, to judge by his body, still
competing on a track real only by inference, by imagining how little
a child needs to see the actual race: cars, track, people filling the

stands: how all it takes is one puny toy. Finally, I rummage out the
clear Elmer's glue, squeeze one drop onto the neck stem, fit the head
back on by wiggling the right crevices together and press down hard
and hold it for about five minutes until it's dry. To this day, you'd
never detect where the neck snapped.

His name still sounds like a flower or a kind of metal or a word from a primitive language, not like a person's name. That, and his intellect in pure Shakespearean lyrics and poems like *Spain, 1937* and the ones about Freud and limestone drew me to him, so I wrote an early Auden trochaic tetrameter rhymed elegy-or-something and sent it with a letter, asking him to let me visit, and soon a note in spidery blue letters on a small square of blue paper came back inviting me to "come to tea" at 4 on a Monday, the day after New Year's Eve, 77 St. Marks Place, New York. I showed up, a seventeen-year-old obsessed with being something, someone; pressed the buzzer, was buzzed in and went up, stepped through the open door on the second floor—vestibule, diningroom, bedroom, kitchen, wide living room and, off the livingroom, a darkened room behind closed French doors with pink panes. Someone, flesh and blood shadow, sat behind those doors, watching, listening. A hulking form, hovering, not quite invisible. An audience whose presence lent judgement or punishment to the scene. A metaphor for something still unknown, unbearable in oneself, that can wound who we think we are in its fury to instruct. Auden waved me to a folding chair placed in front of a grubby white thrift store sectional sofa where he sat and stretched and sidled back and forth. After preliminary chitchat, he asked what kind of furniture my parents owned, he fished for personal data— domestic, trivial, discrete—nothing about poetry, his or mine, nothing intimate enough to distress me though each word and gesture suggested evasions of or probes into the sexual. Everywhere in ashtrays mounds of butts and ashes; plastic utensils, soiled plates, glasses; parts of *The Sunday Times*; books open; scattered fake orientals, some piled on Auden's bed in the bedroom. He needed three or four on top of him at night, their weight "allowed him to sleep." Where the floors showed the wood was dulled with ground-in grime and dust. High ceilings, moldings chipped, wall-to-wall books, spines facing out stacked floor-to-ceiling, nothing but books, no space for a picture, nothing beautiful, treasured or warm, just solid columns of books. A dropleaf table, jumbles of manuscript on it, set up in the middle of the dining area. A typewriter. Two chairs. Auden could finish only six or seven poems a year—"it takes so long to revise." The whole place had the distressed, exhilarating air of work and impermanence, contempt for amenities, of devotion, risk, of mortal makeshift comfort, of someone who feels he doesn't need to belong anywhere—then, I had the idea that this must be the way a saint lives, who cares about *us*, so it doesn't matter how he or his home looks. Rumors claimed he'd attend Salvation Army meetings and write checks for thousands to feed bums. In some ways he looked like a bum—rumpled stained gray suit, skinny gray wrinkled tie, rumpled white shirt, unpressed, unlaundered, un-anything I expected of a great, famous poet. His hair was rough home-cut, fairly short, straight dark straw, his fingernails bitten and bled to the cuticles, like mine in those days, his carpet slippers scuffled when he walked. But he reigned with his face, its deep raw savage creases, chalk skin, sullen nobility; his eyes, fierce close brown agates, could seize you by not blinking or by glancing away as he showed a particle of smile from his gangly six-foot-two height. Let's see, 45 years ago, he would have been about fifty. What hums like silence on the scene is the wraith seated behind those pink-paned doors, dark as the darkness around it, two bright live dots where light collected in pinpoints in faceless eyes, Auden's jealous lover, I know now, sifting each word and gesture of our tryst, presiding over us like one of those unpredictable homicidal gods the Greeks invoked to explain Fate. Auden stood up after awhile and led me to the door. But before I was ushered out, buttoning my raincoat as I turned to leave, back to him, his huge hands covered my shoulders, lingered for a second, then gently pushed me around to face him, slid a thick white pristine envelope—Stephen Spender, ENCOUNTER, the street address, London, typed across its face—into my pocket. "Be a darling, won't you? Mail this for me . . ." I heard and ran down the stairs. In the street I took it out, studied it, wanted to tear it open and read the secret contents of the famous writing to the famous, but I dropped it in the first box I saw. "Lay your sleeping head my love/Human on my faithless arm/Time and Fevers burn away/Individual beauty from/Thoughtless children and the grave/Proves the child ephemeral" whispered inside me in a bar before I caught the train back home to New Jersey, oblivious of what his lines meant, shaken by those eyes behind doors, still held by the hatred of those eyes, if it was hatred, that wordlessly warns and yearns.

When Lowell let me audit his writing course I left New York and rented a furnished room for 7 paltry dollars a week on Boston's exclusive Revere Street. In class he'd read our poems aloud, make a few abrupt shy comments, flirt with a student in the front row, then at the end skulk out fast as if he had committed some unatonable crime. His head was always tilted down a little off to the left as if he held "an invisible violin," ready to play. One day he doesn't show up. Breakdown, another student tells me, he's in MacLean's again. I call his wife, ask if I can see him, and she says fine, he's "only . . . taking a rest." Friday, about three, I enter Bowditch Hall and ask for him. An attendant leads me to his room—American antique: a bed, rope crisscrossed under the horsehair mattress, twin straight-backed spindle chairs, low maple bureau brass handles aglint in the waning winter sun, walnut desk, a drawer on each side pulled out, littered with scrawled-on neatly typed white sheets, finished copies, blanks. Dressed in khaki infantry fatigues, long flapped pockets on the front of the thighs, pea coat and galoshes, I wait in a chair. Soon he's there in the doorway, sweating from squash, white shorts, blue and white striped sailor jersey, flushed, shockingly healthy: he sits on the bed, across from me, facing the windows and the blinding lawns behind me. I sit in a chair, across from him, on the other side of the bed. His small round hornrimmed glasses brim with white light from the sky and lawns, twin mirrors; my tiny anonymous figure sits in them; his flat unyielding powder-blue eyes, faintly visible, seem imbedded in the lenses—it's like seeing myself in another, as another who watches me, a blanked-out unknown self sick with identity, whose instinct is to fuse us both into a permanent thing, make seeing and seen sacred, one. It must be I worship him. All I can do is not comprehend, is be there, stare, wonder. He asks me to listen to new poems from *Life Studies*, reads from the manuscript of drafts stacked in both desk drawers, which poems I can't remember, then asks what I think. "I like the *Lord Weary* poems better," I blurt out, and in his wry self-effacing drawl: "Pound says the book's either genius or pure shit." What do I know? I turn and look outside, making myself part of the silence between us, between the world and us. And all the time the fresh implacable snow darkens in the early twilight, three rows of alien footprints punch the chaste crust, huge tree shadows, blue translucencies, merge with the dimming heavy fall. Then I look back. A fume of rubbing alcohol blossoms, stings my nostrils, instantly fades. I glance across the bed into his eyes, trapped again in those eyes. The white walls, chalky with glare, scary air between us, stun me, I'm not sure who I am or if I'm here, there's nothing inside/outside I can grab to anchor me, the tangible who-we-are-where-we-are flickers, vanishes, seeps back into my known self. More jittery talk. At day end, side by side, we trudge the drifted long front lawn to the high iron gates, their black massive filigreed shields and vines crested with snow. He stops and I walk on, past the gates; he waves a kindly fatherly Goodbye, keeps waving, touched by this petrified mock-son (I think I can see that in his dwindling face) until the street takes me behind a building out of sight and we return, each to his own room. Back in my room with the light off, stretched out on the metal cot, I touch, a foot or so away, desk edge, typewriter, vague white paper mess, lean down, switch on the radio under the bed and, dim yellow glow of the dial rimmed with numbers by my face, tune and tune and tune and tune and tune it.

When a voice said "turn it" that's what I did—turn pain into pleasure, sex into the mad asceticism of the saints, eating into starving, faith into the desolate loss of everything I've always needed, always loved. Then I stood there in bikini underpants squeezing my face in the mirror, making ape grimaces, flexing my arms, admiring the thick white hair on my chest, posing like an athlete so I wouldn't think of myself as a short, helpless Jew. I found along the mirror's edge areas of rotted silver—I could see through to a fragment of wall, or recall the erratic withering of flower petals or imagine the window to a second world where nothing needs to see itself before it dies the way we do. I pressed against the sink, leaned forward, studied every stain of the glass's decay, forgot my face and body. Then "turn it" came again, and I took the gilt-framed antique mirror in both hands, lifted it down a few inches onto the sink and turned it around. The twisted wires it had hung on were frayed, there were faint wobbly scrawls in what looked like a child's handwriting—"hidden myself here" "who never speaks" "who cannot die" "pity" "whose face is the" "except this" "with Go (faded) unfor (faded)" "leave un(faded)"—plus, on the dry cracked brown paper backing, three water stains shaped like a woman's kisses, lips open.

Some say acceptance is the heart of it, or grief, the "true self," or the
here-and-now, some say it's the "I" behind the infinite realm of
selves the "I" is, but who knows who one is, why and how one is?
Sometimes a sentence lets us know, like Johnson's "Speake that I
may see thee," sometimes a blunt command like that reminds us of
something we did because of what it says we wanted to let the world
know, do for the world, for ourselves, reveal in a form which, at the
time, we didn't realize was the only form. I am a Jew. I am a faithless,
sinfully selfish Jew. No. Not that. I am also kind and tender. And
enraged and bitter. No. Loving. Not that. Withdrawn and fright-
ened. Generous and wild. Obscene. Heroic—no definitely not that.
Innocent, saintly and meek. I am a Jew, and on one particular
Halloween 35 years ago I decided to wear a Hitler costume, make it
myself. I picked out my wife's red wool mini-skirt, an old olive drab
Army jacket, white button-down Brooks shirt, black knitted tie and
rubber boots, and mascaraed that famous stub of a moustache on my
upper lip, pasted my hair across forehead and showed up at the party
we were invited to. The thing to consider is the feeling, how I felt
that night living behind the identity of a stranger, how true to him
I was, how true to myself, why I chose to be him. Or not. No. Not
that. I am a Jew. I wore that costume as a Jew, I wanted to mirror
his murderous depraved self, the effeminate Nazi coward behind the
mobs and slaughters. And yet at times I've heard that selfsame
twittering whiny voice in my own head, an imitation of an imitation,
heterosexual me imitating the finicky artificiality of the queen.
Sometimes I hear it at the mirror, shaving, fueled by anger, as other
voices have behind them an as-yet-unidentified emotion-event con-
nected to no one, made less dangerous that way, so the voice, always
an anonymous voice, is a mask for the feeling, for something we
believe is terrible about ourselves: as if behind who we are—
"identity" is our favorite word for it—as if back "there" an infinite

self actually is everyone in the pure possibility of identity—that skin or image I call Steve—as if who we are isn't much more than a social grace, a bow to the necessity of getting along in life. As if, after all, the "I" is mere interpretation. But not that either. Not that. Not anything I understand. Unless this fantasy explains it—at the party, I enjoyed wearing a skirt, having my cock and balls swing free, no underpants, above the open airy hem of the skirt. Is that how women feel? I mean, is there a special, brutal hint of freedom and power in having one's crotch so easily entered by the world, so vulnerable? I know how good it is when a woman you love slips her hand into your pocket and hunts for your penis. I remember a girl I loved in New York who never wore underpants so whenever I was with her or whenever she crossed my mind it was impossible not to see her dark thing, bearded and moist, laid over the world. I wish I could explain what it was to mimic that mad asshole. Did he dress up, too, at his coke-high private parties, mincing in front of his officers and girlfriends, flipping up his skirt, in full lipstick and rouge, mooning his captive audience whenever its interest waned, ordering his frozen worshippers to find an accurate name for him, his right, real name, and as each one called out his guess, screaming like a baby back at them—"NO. NOT THAT! NOT THAT!"

Behind me, the blank world; in front of me what I see—buildings, streets, lush trees, distance, tattered clouds, a glimpse of brilliant water, her, him, it—always the absolute absence of God. I stand between, almost like a mirror facing a mirror, and "almost" is the key: I'm almost here. "We are lost in childhood," Sartre moans, and I believe it, but what does it mean? Rimbaud stopped writing poetry at eighteen, edging toward madness, then chose the world of business, where prophetic song doesn't mean shit, where the words "visionary" and "apocalyptic" make people laugh, where speech isn't risked to explore mind until words pierce the lost layer of community, of the need to commune, though that's where the illuminations in his new poems took him. He wears a belt of gold dust and the weight of it causes sores and chafes his organs until they bleed. That's the main fact for me—how he converted poetry into gold, about $40,000.00 worth lugged through jungle and desert until a tumor of the knee stops him and he's taken by litter to Harar, then Roche, Paris, Marseille, too late to save his life. From his diary: ". . . stretched out, with my leg bandaged, tied, retied, changed, in such a way that I cannot move it. I've become a skeleton: I'm an object of fear. My back is all sore from the bed; I can't sleep a minute and it has grown terribly hot here. . ..The litter is already half dislocated and the people completely done in. I try to mount a mule, with my sick leg tied to its neck; I have to get off after a few minutes and return to the litter, which is already a kilometer behind. Arrived at Balawa. It's raining. Furious wind all night." Then there's the eerie early Carjat photo of him. Wispy, fuming with adolescent disgust and girlish disdain, already adept at "the sterility of genius," at wasting one life and starting another, he peers off into space from an affliction that says we have no right to be here, as we are, not conscious enough of our fate, of our debt to the cosmos, trapped in civilization's blind lust for the factory, for goods, for the machine, for the destruction of life that should be lived in "the key of love." One feels at times, listening to his vatic arias—pain laminating pain into one premonitory wail—that his vicious tenderness, his ache to annihilate and save the world, clash in eternal simultaneous splendor, that they exist with such force because he knows desire never can find what it needs, it goes on burning us, an inner hell forever, like the sick leg that killed him, like the universe itself. "La musique savant manque à notre désire," he announces in *L'Illuminations*: No music can fully reveal who and how we are—our infinitely shifting selves and faces, our fear of being no one, souls hoping, flailing, thirsting, searching each other for what has no name, as if God placed an invisible veil between each of us, between ourselves and ourselves, between us and Him, that can't be breached or clarified though we keep trying to break through—into ourselves, into others—Jesus, what silences we contain. They take his leg at the knee. "Shit to poetry," he screams at one of the doctors, poking his head in to chat.

For Jerry

Here's one of those warm simple letters in that big six-year-old
scrawl of yours, filling the whole page with your statement, clear,
sweet, kind, associating values with detail with Nietzsche with the
glory of poetry with some local flower or creature you bumped into
yesterday and fell in love with, with the expensive tweed coat I gave
you last time you were here. "Jews understand coats, life-giving
coats, protection against death," you say in the letter, and "It's easy
being crazy when the house is empty, thinking of birds of prey
wearing black hats." Jerry, the yellow Irish raglan-shoulder coat I
bought with money my father gave me is yours now, it's draped on
your beefy Hebrew shoulders in the sticks, near Easton, PA, where
nobody has good taste, nobody will admire its nubby unassuming
weave, its hand-loomed itchy grain brimming with dots of pink.
Where you live it's as if cities don't exist yet, all's primitive, all's
survival. And none of them know shit about coats—their cloudy
bone buttons and waxed thread sewn crisscross over and over until
there's a sharp lump the owner can rub his thumb across for comfort.
It's a Burberry, you schmuck, and you probably couldn't care less. It
didn't fit from the day I picked it out, its long tent-like form comes
from the past of animal pelts and capes and blankets with a slit cut
in the middle, for living in nature not the city where people love
clothes that "enhance" the body. Russians know coats, don't they?
And Jews, those death-fearing, Godless, touchy maniacs of the world
who need their vulnerable, paranoid bodies ecstatic, wrapped in a
heavy expensive coat—so gas fumes can't penetrate, so torture cuffs
can't swell their ankles and wrists, so the ideas of clean rigid Gentiles
who believe in social justice, in eliminating obstructions to justice,
can't get in, so the hands of strangers on a bus or in a street crowd
can't reach their delicate skin, so even the hands of tender love can't
change their mood. Eliot, Pound and Joyce bought themselves coats,
showed off gorgeous Isle of Skyes, Meltons, Sheared Camel Hairs,

hoping it would drop below zero just to test how absolute their coats were, whether they were true mortal coats that could give life, define life, save life. What a Jewish idea! But I believe it. A coat so well-made, so heavy and fine, it could actually prevent death: an immortality coat! Right now I want my coat back, Jerry, even though it's late May; it's the only coat I know that might help me to live forever, but I give myself a stupid effeminate kiss in the long bathroom mirror down to my crotch, and, instead, lather and shave, a kiss instead of a coat, and the sadness of how much I'll miss that sack of stitched woven wool come December takes over. Naked, I shave, an hour before leaving to teach, zipping the blue plastic Good News across cheek over chin up to the lip under a nostril, and it strikes me that I should lecture on coats today, not poetry, inspired by the coat I gave you, which has probably fallen off its cheap wire hanger by now, a blurred heap among gashed rubber boots, the vacuum cleaner, outgrown ice skates, twisted hats and whatever else you've chucked down there to be sold at a yard sale. My lecture should explain the coat's power to stop death and somehow should represent divine coats in an act that uses a real coat. I'll wear one of my coats to class. I walk in. Take out my note cards, still wearing my coat. I keep it on. Suddenly it's quiet. I'm talking about the coat, your coat, all coats. Brilliant. Euphoric. Letting my mind speak, wandering in honest blindness. Then I add, "Lusting for a hundred things this morning, I'd rather have a coat than anything, deep, unassailable cloth to shield a back and chest on a cold night so securely that the man who wears it feels he can stand anything, do anything, survive even his own death, grateful for the feel of it, for the weight, for the reassuring dense goodness against his hands, for the shiny fragrant trace of natural oil it leaves in a film on his palms and fingers." Then I call one student up and draw her inside my coat by opening it, like Dracula, still lecturing, and button us in and feel her jump when my crazy stiff dick springs and pulses against her belly, still lecturing on coats, whispering, declaiming, making scholarly digressions, invoking history, origins, fashion, textures, hissing out of the side of my mouth to her—"Stay calm, don't let anybody know,"—as her hand slips it in a little and I sway, finishing, asking questions, answering questions, blithely in touch with their faces as she comes, three or four muffled tremors, all this time both our faces turned toward the class while she twitters as if the whole thing's merely a lecture on coats. "What a beautiful coat you have," she says, "so roomy, warm." I thank her for the compliment and say, "You should see the one I gave Jerry," unable to recall one thing I've said to the class during the last few minutes. Ah, this life, which even the best coat can't protect us from; this death, too strong for the warmest coat there is. Nevertheless, some coats will never let us die—I know it. Every time I step into the hall closet and sniff its musty dark and rove my hands over the coats—first shoulders, sleeves, then the long drape of the body—awed by their softness, and caress mine, I pray it's one of those coats, the holy ones. I close the door and stay there, as long as I can, blindly nuzzling and singing.

The difference between death and the individual is the gaze...

—Giacometti

Taped up over my desk, a bust of Giacometti's mistress. Unconsolably alive to the moment, nostrils flared upward and out, her crucified eyes seem fixed on some catastrophe, her white lips breathe. They'd sit in his 17 x 27 studio, walls splashed gray, swarming with plaster dust, and stare at each other for hours. She'd pose, or simply sit there. They'd meet almost every day for years. It became their ritual for what each needed from the other, because of the salvation they imagined waited in the other—the sense of being held, heard, seen, in the acceptance of non-possessive love. Snapshots of them together (my favorite's in a bar) show he never smiles. He keeps his famous hangdog air. Cropped dark hair, bright innocent carnal grin, she's always beaming in the naive ecstatic denials of youth. What transpires in the studio is sacred: they scour each other's eyes incessantly to find out what they feel, understand, believe; they pray something will explode them into The Real; they rarely speak—this gorgeous-when-first-met 19-year-old prostitute, Carolyn, and her artist-friend, near 60, consumed with capturing the human head, who moans he'll never sculpt a head the way he sees it, ("I do not care if a work is good or not," he writes), who suddenly sees walking as "moments of immobility," and from then on is horrified by the miracle of standing, moving, being alive. He can't sleep unless he groups his socks and shoes by his bed in just the right, different pattern each night. He tosses millions of lira from sales under an old couch. He gives money to anyone who asks. Once, for four straight months, all he can think about is ". . .burning myself alive at 4 o'clock in the morning on the sidewalk in front of my studio." He can't stop rehearsing it. He's terrified he'll do it. He buys a full can of gasoline, plants it in the middle of his studio, sits there, sniffs the fumes, can't stop analyzing the unique practical shape of the red metal.

For four months I worked as a chauffeur in Mexico City for Hal B. Hayes. I was on a writing grant, it was our honeymoon; one of our friends, Octavio, a tourist guide and driver, heard Hayes was looking for a driver and knew I needed money. I called, went to his hotel on The Reforma—a penthouse suite—and he hired me, gave me plane tickets to L.A. the next day to pick up his new black Caddie stretch limo and two female friends plus a list of personal belongings at his house. The driveway climbed past a mazey stucco grotto painted blue, blue water and caves, exotic fronds, potted at irregular points on the bottom. A butler let me in. Wall controls at the touch of a switch would lift the rugs against nuclear attack, cover the high picture windows on three sides. Soon his man came back and handed me a leather satchel, which I opened to check: 100 blue plastic baby combs, black pearl cufflinks from Zsa Zsa (his wife-to-be), sex vitamins, a manual on how to set up blind trusts, guidebooks, shoe laces, ties, etc. In one of the upstairs bathrooms a fifty foot long wall-length closet bulged with a row of suits, grouped by color, at least eighty or ninety pairs of shoes shone like big toy cars lined up on a wire rack an inch above the floor. I drove the car back to my hotel, The Biltmore, Pershing Square, Sunday—leftwing Christian lunatics raving, carrying signs—had a few drinks and went to sleep. Next morning I picked up Hayes's friends, the two women dressed to the teeth in silk dresses, jewelry, heels, tinted hair, make-up done so thick and vivid it looked like icing. Bursts of acidic perfume. Doris Day voices. Giggling, as they slid their tight sleek asses onto the leather. Luggage stashed in the trunk, we took off for the border. The plains of Mexico up north are dry, weary, dignified, numb, scrub, cactus, hills scalloping the distance, faded brown, now and then flowers, streaks of grass, elated sorrow coming in whiffs, little airy wisdoms approximating joy coming from the self, coming from the land, a sense that out there in the emptiness man doesn't matter any more than the earth matters to itself. Look up and it's all endless famous blue, clarity, crisp bright air, always a chill in it. Death scents, pungent mixtures of plants, dirt, dung, absences, silence, space—strange to be riding in that car, then and there, strange to be me. Sometimes we'd buzz through one of the dusty sleepy villages past a red coke cooler and its knot of people, scare chickens, dogs, a farmer or kid walking the road, leading a donkey cart, and once one of my silly passengers tossed a sandwich out the window—to help, she thought, an old campesino squatting on the roadside, scooping water out of a ditch with a tin can. Through my window raindrops approaching from beyond the hills caught my cheek. Back in Mexico City driving for Hayes became a weird day-long near-fantasy routine. The first day I showed up for work I was told to wait in one of the bedrooms of his suite. A man in a dark blue suit was eating breakfast. He had a skeletal, yellowish face, a short order cook's face. I introduced myself: he introduced himself and told me he was Hayes's "full-time pimp." That day I drove Hayes out to a hidden golf club in the suburbs, waited a few hours, as usual, taking notes, trying to write poetry, anything to justify my image of myself as a poet. When he got back I asked how it went and I remember his: "I bought it." He stepped into the back, I got in, and as always he pulled out the miniature twinkling bar tucked into the back of the driver's seat—its crystal tumblers and decanters recessed in silver trays, the surface of its varnished fold-down walnut shelf a mirror—and poured himself a full glass of gin. All day long he'd drink until by nightfall he was like a rubber doll, slurring the simplest words, collapsing into stupor. Five days a week at nine I'd report and wait to take him somewhere, to bribe this official or that, to start a hotel then stop it at the girders and floors stage. There he was, this self-made redneck South Carolina boy, who made mud bricks with his hands as a kid and worked his way up to building barracks for the

Air Force, office buildings, hotels, who rarely spoke, blue blazer, pearl gray flannel pants, blue shirt, striped rep tie and cordovan loafers. His silence was ominous. Whether it was blindness or reticence or inarticulate fury about something he could never reveal, I can't say. It was vicious like the hollow pause before a storm breaks when the air hesitates and nothing breathes. One night I took him "home"—he was renting a house as well as the suite—and instead of leaving after he went in, I snuck up to one of the living room windows and waited. He stood there, arms at his sides, dangling a bottle in his hand; then a lovely dark-haired girl, the maid, I guess, came up to him, talking about nothing I could hear, and he dropped to his knees, clung to her legs and seemed to beg, beg, until she stepped back—he had thrust both hands up her dress—and kicked off his arms and left him weeping on the floor. I remember an image in my mind of his numb genitals, of a blunt blank fist-like crotch or ridge made of nothing but bone. A few days later he called me into the living room of his suite and asked me to read a speech he had written for a business club. It was strong, practical prose, short sentences, everything in the present, unmistakably superficial, about money—it's value, how to make it—five pages long. The last paragraph, though, where he raves, extolling money and religion, yoking them, defining the sacred meaning of cash, cursing most men's understanding of money, explaining how to make millions, proving that a man who amasses wealth is holy, heroic, like a great general, like "someone from Homer," ends, I have to admit, with one overwhelming sentence, clinching his argument—"Money is God in circulation." What else? In flight from the U.S. Govt. because he had built substandard airforce base barracks that collapsed and pocketed money he should have used to build them properly, this silly, empty man, a fugitive, didn't move me at all then, not consciously. I was 24, just married, having a high time writing, travelling, bumming around, not ready to face who I was. I was a naive witness to his demise. Now that my own slide downward has begun, I've seen how chance and choice can ruin you, can maim you permanently, tilt the delicate array of mind, how things change and you have to work like a maniac inside your head to see life a new way, you have to build a whole new attitude to survive. Hayes was already caught in the slide, but he managed to look elegant each morning, sober, perfectly dressed after his barber came to shave him, trim his hair. Once, one late afternoon, the women I had delivered from California visited his suite. We had just returned from Acapulco where he was trying to finish a hotel—zoning problems, legal problems, were holding it up. From my room across the hall, I watched them enter his room: a glass filled with ice and gin tinkled in his hand. They shut the door. Muffled banter and laughter trickled through the door and, about an hour later, an hour of relative silence, the ladies came out and one of them tittered to the other passing my door, "Christ, after all that work he couldn't even get it up!" Soon, after that, he fired me for running a red light and crushing the door of a Mexican's old muffin-like Nash. I missed the great Hayes. It was like being an extra in a movie about the American dream, like actually being in the dream, or whatever you call a nobody-from-nowhere's rise to the top—engaged to a movie star with big tits, mega-rich, keeping his own pimp and barber. He often grumbled about going bald, he believed those baby blue combs with fine delicate teeth would help retard it. His personal barber would arrive for the daily shave and haircut, spend one full hour keeping his hair the same length, refining, hair by hair, his hair, to stop it from growing at all. That's how Hayes wanted it. The barber would always use a blue baby comb. I could hear (sitting with the pimp) the scissors' precise *hiss hiss* pass across words whispered between them as the blades crisscrossed in tight flourishes near his head, as the barber, like some mustachioed comical maestro in a white apron, stood there, elbows out, intently shaping the world's most perfect haircut, making sure not one single strand had been missed, again and again, pinched between index and middle fingers, obsessively measuring the length so it came out absolutely even everywhere, most of the time, I'm sure, cutting air.

For Louise Glück

I'll never forget—a newspaper photograph of the tunnel, excavated
by archaeologists, running between the hilltop monastery and the
convent a half mile below: hundreds of newborns propped up in
alcoves like dolls, they each looked slightly different, a kind of
ancestral personality, a destiny shaping their bodies and faceless
skulls, those never-to-be children in the wall of secrecy, of lust's
complex piety, standing at attention across half the front page of *El
Diario*, so close their skeleton elbows touched, so well-preserved
their bones—jaw, scapula, ankle, spine—pressed into dirt seemed
to reach out, seemed like the blueprints of souls. From our street of
shops in San Angel on that hill, the monastery's white walls, gate
and gilded dome, crowned by a simple cross in euphoric Mexicano
light against pure blue; the clean yeasty bouquet of fresh rolls, beef
sides and gutted pigs on hooks, hair swept into fluffy piles. Our
bedroom looked out through glass doors onto a patio and sky; from
the roof Popocatéptl's white-peaked glory. Each dawn a band—
trumpet, guitar, drums—in the market behind our place would
wake us like a human alarm clock. We'd lie there, listening. Its cheap
noise made us happy.

The three of us are waiting for his plane, sitting and drinking in one of the airport bars, surveying the field of jets nosed close to the building, mechanics' carts scooting between planes, parked fuel trucks, hoses stuck into fuselages, wide sky, weak hazy blue, horizon pimpled with trees and buildings. His coming carries echoes of his books, the 60s drugs and turmoil, war, assassinations, us in our 30s trying to raise kids, the clash of marriage and "freedom," body with mind, his cold intricate nearly intolerable dissection of relationships, collusion, fear-bred love, and back of it the family's awesome silent script of dependencies like a Greek myth determining as we choose, being chosen as we determine. Short, muscular, slightly stooped, beak nose and charming smile, the man deplanes and glides up the ramp to the lobby. We all shake hands. He's shy but firm, self-contained, slightly nervous, groggy from the last few days in Colorado, a yellow enamel and gold Naropa pin stuck to his tan corduroy jacket lapel. We go downstairs, wait for his luggage (one suitcase jammed with books feels like a hundred pounds), then Bill, Margot and I, and Laing, walk to the car and drive back to Philadelphia, where Laing and others will speak at a symposium—*World Peace and The Individual.* In the car nobody says much. At his hotel we agree to meet in an hour at Dilullo's for a drink then eat dinner somewhere. Laing shows up at the bar, his breath blows peppermint toothpaste, we have a few, then go off to The Garden, one of the good restaurants here. All the time we're together, I confess, I expect something special from the man, but that act of projection we devise in the presence of celebrity—making the other radiate secret wisdom which if only we knew would change our lives, kill our pain, solve everything—seems not to work. We're just three people chatting, getting a little drunk, telling stories, slowly becoming a few degrees more intimate. Naturally, Laing remains the one among us who has something we need, and he does not give it, which may be

The Last Lesson, who knows, and we order more drinks, and go on talking. I think Bill asks about schizophrenia and Laing tells us about being a shrink in the Army hanging out with locked-up psychotics and how he discovered they weren't all that different from us, they could form "a warm bond" and didn't seem to want or need treatment—that was the point Laing made, he decided that treatment wasn't what he wanted to do to people who were "sick." No doubt we talked about other things, especially Love, tried other ways to find out what he thought. He had nine children and wanted more, as many as possible, and planned to move back to Scotland. Married twice. Exhibits a clear sense of discretion in public. Balding, white hair on sides of head. Deep lines scoring each cheek, strong nose, not tall, not big but stocky. Often drifts into himself, is incommunicative, seems unaware of surroundings, inappropriate grimaces, smiles, then returns to a sociable steady give-and-take. We order wine and food and talk more, and either Laing or I bring up mothers. I tell him I've just sent my mother three Art Tatum records, she likes to listen to jazz and plays it herself on the piano. I sketch some of the mother-and-son problems we've had but revise to the present, now, when, it would certainly seem, she and I get along pretty well. 77. She must die soon. Sad. Very sad. Then Laing tells us about his last visit to his "stiff, Calvinist, unemotional" mother, a few years back. He and a couple of his kids visit her in Scotland and "seem to have a good time" although she's "cold," as usual, "distant." Four months later, after they've returned home, Laing gets a letter from his mother saying, "Dear Ronald, I want you to promise never to visit me again, and that you won't visit my grave, ever." Those are his actual words. I ask him what he did. He says, "Well, I took out a sheet of paper," (his voice very calm, his brogue gravelly now), "drew a big heart on it, and wrote, 'I promise,' inside the heart, and sent it to her. That was quite awhile ago. Haven't seen her since. Don't know whether she's dead or alive." For a minute I can't tell whether he's told that story as a parable to teach me about myself—his lack of concern for her, or for himself, his apparent lack of guilt, shock me. I still wonder if the story applies to me. But really it's his problem, not mine. I mean, the fact is, my mother did say similar things to me, but we've made up and are friendly. It pleases me to hear what she does, how her new stereo makes her happy, though sometimes I'm not sure. . .odd—at the airport, waiting for him to land, I skim through his book about the politics of the family, or maybe the recent one where religion creeps in, and stumble on a passage that chills me: "We are acting parts in a play we have never read and never seen, whose plot we don't know, whose existence we can glimpse, but whose beginning and end are beyond our present imagination and conception," then glance up from the page to the long clean silver jets lifting off, diminishing, touching down, taxiing, parked side by side diagonally along the huge glass wall, not a face visible behind the wee passenger windows.

It sits on top of an old shadeless gooseneck in his tailorshop window, a lone light showing nothing, a beacon leading no one anywhere. Maybe he put it there to ward off thieves, maybe to remind himself of what he was when he bent over pants and jackets, sewing buttons, fixing the torn cloth. I was walking home up the long gentle 20th Street hill to my house on Mt. Vernon when I saw the smudged bleak window, nothing in it except the bulb atop its jointed metal stem, no more than 40 watts. I stopped for a minute, stood in the evening street, thought of the man it belonged to. I see him taking a walk some days, in his eighties, using an old cane, up 20th, obviously going nowhere, blank eyes focused on a distance with nothing in it. I see him sitting in his window above the empty first floor shop where the bulb is, a wall of books behind him, watching TV, the weak blue amoeba-like glare of the screen squirming on his face. Over the years he's gotten fatter, slowed, walks more bent over, looking down at the pavement, leaning on his cane. Each night the bulb's on, a mundane star crowning a skinny spine. The bulb is merely itself, but tonight—I'm not sure why—it means something impossible to explain. "When I was born, sixty-three years ago. . ." Would those words help me to express. . .a question, the sketch of a question? In a small brown photograph, torn off across the bottom, unearthed by my daughter, Clair, from an album, my thirteen-year-old mother— name and date faded on the back—sits hugging a white puppy in her lap on the front steps of the family's West Philadelphia working class row house. I've studied it almost every morning for the last three years and still can't define what I see. Summer. The puppy's tongue curls out. Can a dog smile? Its white coat and her white blouse merge. Her cheek pressed against the dog's cheek, she looks down. Sun bleaches the wooden steps she sits on, railing, column, porch behind her head, segment of gleaming hair; some cruel mood of the light embodies. . . . What remains after the girl, dog, man, are gone? What would be in her eyes if she looked up?

You think you know but you don't, you try, you use words, you
actually speak, you put your head in your right hand, hand against
cheek, you rub your gum, pick your nose, smooth hair back, anger
seethes under something, you, you, you, you sit there alone, trying
to figure it out, your mind—unhelped by all the beloved characters
you've read about, refer to—simply drones on as you, as the you
writing and reading, look up with a tilt of the head resembling
prayer at a skyscraper's massive zigzag commercial blue neon crown
ignite the evening air, and the emptiness, the civilized thinking, a
skin pulled tight across the violences of desire and absurd laws you
were born to, begins to simmer, the underside of you begins to break
you down again into yourself, the truth-starved wail you carry and
don't know how to quite find and express except in sex or argument
or hatred of past wrongs, you are you, and you and you, but who?
and the idea of the angelic unleashes itself, of the devil swathed in
a cloak of wealth descends from someone's penthouse, of a memory
of rejection by someone you couldn't touch, of money, death or
whatever, you think you know but it's impossible to be *and* to know,
being is not knowing, is dying too soon, stomach, teeth, kneecap,
eyesight, tendonitis, and the amazing dream—because of its clarity
of possession, its self-propelled mania, its intact innate meaning no
brain can unravel, carried in your jacket pocket—is beautiful and
can save you. You wrote these words down when you woke: I am
travelling through a wooded realm but people wilderness perhaps
but not completely people are around and I come on some people
they're vague and pleasant and Millie is in the scene but also vague
or borne in a gelatinous casing she's ill and someone wipes away the
jelly that's on her face now clearly her and she opens eyes slightly
and says a few kind disjointed words I turn away and when I turn
back she's dead her face is very still and peaceful then I go deeper
into the woods along a road or field and come to a narrow passageway

with no woods just a sort of gentle ramp with a pale blue door at the
top of it I ask someone how to go through he reaches up and takes
a hidden key from inside a complicated raw hole in a wall and opens
the blue door it slides apart at the middle slow slow a precipice
beyond which there is nothing but mist infinite distance a wall
shreds moving across appears like a proof of eternity it's "the edge
of the universe" or "the end of the world" space yearning phrases I
see the tips of my shoes protrude over the brink into this never
known as real as any ordinary day and I turn back not horrified not
appalled child-like awed given something overwhelmingly rare
sure I'll have to tell my daughter Margot about Millie my wife's
death I keep my feelings to myself go back on the road stop in a
restaurant-bar somehow I have been given a handful of white pills
so I'll be okay I'm at the bar talking asking about the route back and
finally confess Millie's death and in this dream break down sob
woefully long in grief racked then go my way recalling a spongy
stretch ahead earlier I avoided went around sob the last dregs out
and wake—use this if you can, tell it to yourself until it bores you,
maybe it's the key to the place where all the answers throb right
there in the belly the way you wrote this down when you wakened
and recited it to fix that image, redemptive of all the heart is
shriveled by—blue door opening onto nothing onto the infinity the
soul feels in its airy gut always but cannot say or sing, all the soul
collides with, must kiss, must embrace when its own piteous voice
of faith in the world seeks resurrection.

I

Upper lip, lower lip, cheek, neck, sideburn, chin, the wet charcoal of
stubble cut under the creamy foam, waking the face is like a wound
healing, known again, recognized, disdained, refamiliarized, the
you-I/I-you seeks its other with "It's me!" in a gleeful identification
of the self that can never be the person, be the identity at the bottom
that's there, we know, because we feel it every day as feeling. It is a
miracle, this being here, this you, this me, this nothing
except . . . darkness is behind my face like a cold field, no stars out,
darkness is behind the bathroom mirror like a black sky with
nothing behind it . . . and the freshmown hairs whisper their crisp
phrase, their empty consolation. . .and all this time, taken for granted
in the glass, I shave, wash, check for missed spots, re-shave closer,
rinse ears, rub mask . . . I own a Guatemalan mask, bittersweet
chocolate-brown, carved, milky white faint fine undersized ears
scratched into the wood abnormally high above the hairline where
the thick wood ends and the face evaporates. Nothing and no one
moves behind the face, unless it's whatever part of the world hap-
pens to be there behind it. Its slit eyes only see if you hold it against
your face; its mouth is a pained frozen frown; its beaked nose is a
blade—all say life's barely possible, life's intolerable, life's an edge
of some kind we can't step back from but must. Through its own
shallow blindness light pours through; the world in front and behind
pours through this shell of its existence—everything on the front
fully there, everything on the back there as well, no thought
between to interfere, so like one of those heartbreaking Russian
concerto violin solos I've heard blossom all at once hundreds of times
and love because it brings tears, because in it emotion swells,
completes me and belongs as I belonged to myself in childhood . . .
I comb wet hair, sleek eyebrows down, look away, look back, blink,
close tight, open, relax my eyes closed and keep my eyes closed and
want to keep my eyes closed.

II

The three profile self-portraits Sidney Goodman charcoaled evolve to the death of self, the leaps from one to two, from two to three, magnify his head, frame it with a scrawled line then finally explode in a blur of blood as he staunches it and draws so close to the mirror his nose touches it, merges with it, the face thicker deeper black than the first two, the features less important, the loss of cautious mowing across the cheek planes and chin replaced by the fury of mutilation. One pale diagonal white scar still shows on my chin where flesh once caught as it humped ahead of the impatient blade that left an eighth-of-an-inch furrow. What kind of love is this? In a fantasy of salvation once I thought I felt myself absolutely neither the seer nor the seen—both at once—nothing but the one untouchable image floating just inside the glass. The outside me, the one one usually knows is real, was gone, and all that stood where I was was the universe, the steamy white tile universe and beyond. Then the him that was me in the mirror, and the me that was fully me, fleshed, finished shaving, washed, took a shower, dressed and walked outside to do errands: bank, laundry, air-conditioning repair service, buy polaroid, coffee and muffin. That night, light off, back home, standing in the dark bathroom for a piss, I peeked into the same clear rectangular glass. It was twilight, the room seemed soaked in haze, and what I saw was someone indistinct, some anybody or nobody only vaguely like myself, though I knew it had to be me. I stood there, hoping for more, wishing redefinition for the bare incurable self.

III

How close the face is, mirror is face, face mirror in a storm of cloudy black, the raw smeared beard both blur and beard, pencil and hair, vacuous metaphor, imageless image, inconsequential insight. Blood. A rag. A vacant torso. Dark dark head. A lesson? Reprimand? A final self, untouchable and fleshless? The abstract accidental short black stroke that hangs in the air behind his head like a fate quirk, the sleepworn eyes half-heeding the blade, the hand either stopping the blood with a cloth or raised simply to finish shaving—impossible to tell—space raving between the man stripped to the waist and the face he ponders in the glass trying not to cut himself though he does cut himself in haste or hatred or a crazy slip. . .no way to tell from the drawing. The background empty behind the empty torso.

IV

"Be like an empty cave," commands Hakuin.

"The blurred bloodrush of self-loathing and loving" as I stand here each day watching myself age makes me want to punch the face in the glass, punch everything that is, punch death in myself that I can't reach, admit, accept, reconcile, no matter how deeply I believe I could be saved if I could only. . . I remember when I stood staring at myself in a small downstairs bathroom mirror one spring morning. One beautiful morning. It doesn't matter why, but I kept staring until the man staring and the man he stared at in the glass jumped in and out of existence, the mirror image would disappear for an instant, I seemed to evaporate too, then I'd unfocus and the mirror me would intensify, be all I was for so long terror forced me to come back tensed against the sink edge, refusing to disengage from the empty replica of myself that would become more real than I was when I really concentrated on nothing but what I saw out there in the chrome-rimmed medicine cabinet mirror until both of us disappeared, only *tick tick tick tick*, like that, wisps of insect noise, hints of identity. Death snarls on my lips, love loosens my ties to myself, gives me back to myself, and between them the touch of deathless meaning. In Scythia, when a king died, at the end of the year they'd take fifty of his best servants, strangle and gut them, stuff the bodies with chaff, and sew them up again. These men were native Scythians. Fifty top horses were then subjected to the same. The next step was to cut a number of wheels in half and fix them in pairs, rim downwards, to stakes driven into the ground, two stakes to each half-wheel; then stout poles are driven lengthwise through the horses from tail to neck, and by means of these horses are mounted on the wheels, so that the front pairs support the shoulders and the rear pairs the belly between the thighs. All four legs are left dangling clear of the ground. Each horse bitted and bridled, the bridle led forward and pegged down. The bodies of the men are dealt with in a similar way: straight poles are driven up through the neck, parallel with the spine; the lower protruding ends are fitted into sockets in the stakes which run through the horses. Thus each horse is provided with one of the young servants to ride him. When horses and riders are all in place around the tomb, they're left there, and the mourners go away. This ancient ritual—what does it mean, how did it quiet death? In the bedroom where my wife and I usually sleep, lights off, late last night I sat with my mother. We spoke of her dying, of her cancer, both our faces smudges in the room, our faces part of the darkness. She touched my arm. "What does that mean?" I asked. "What do you think it means?" she said. We were talking before she went to sleep, to help her sleep. Now and then, when she would sob, I'd place my left hand on her head and smooth her hair, just to touch her, just to have her be touched.

B U R N I N G

For Riki Wagman

Neighbors had made a garden out of a small lot on the corner and were digging furrows, planting seeds, nailing up stakes and chick-enwire, the barbershop was there, its short plump owner dozed as usual in one of his two leather and porcelain chairs, his old TV churned its flimsy images, the Russian Orthodox church was closed except for the wing where the homeless lived, dropped my letters in the mailbox near Black & Decker across from the Juvenile Detention Center and 9th district station, passed the hot dog and pretzel man by the library, strolled around Logan Square's Calder fountain by the Museum of Natural History, the huge bronze breasts and thighs of the goddesses gleaming water, Four Seasons, limos, Cigna, up 18th to Rittenhouse, it was all there as before, and why not, sweat started on my palms and forehead when I realized This is all there is, it began and it will end, they say, this is all there is, it is burning, birth death like a palace of leaves, burning, saw dogshit clog my cleated sole scraped it off on a curb then on grass by a tree, then used a twig, the hundred different quartz watches, buttons, displays, black and silver, in the electronics shop across from Pour Vous, Sue's Fruits and Vegetables with its packed stalls juice machine customers, Rindelaub's restaurant now nothing but a cheap bakery, even the faeces, even Christ, even the cracked fucked-up pavement under my feet, the gift of its drab heart (pray? should I pray?) burning—these must have told me what I had always known in my prideful terrors, but I can't say, only God who needs no God can, or insects communicating their next move, or the pulse of a leaf—every building, shopper, car and garbage can erupting with the praise and grace of existence, a kind of delirious grief in gratitude for the possibility of existence, who yearning for who yearning for who, it was weird—instantly I resisted, windowshopped, studied books skirts shoes, watched faces, did my interminable shit-scared cretin philosophy, calculated by the feel of bills in my pocket if I had enough for lunch, any appointments?—but it was happening: picture yourself caused by light witnessed by light stated by the throat of light redeemed by light.

Those glum, blank-faced, two-, three-storey row houses in Philly
on the fringes of slums in starved light, glare, look as if layers of
hope have been peeled off, nearly to the bone, a soreness constant
as air hurts everything from dogs to storefronts to the tilt, sag and
precarious mortar of old walls and chimneys. Another layer off and
the lath would show. Even in summer a chill reeks from unknown
sources, existence is a cracked plate glass window, the hardness of
an oak school desk chair, a door lock held on by a single screw, a
man leaning against a chain link parking lot fence, pushing his
cheek against the cold squares of wire. He wears a tan poplin jacket
and oil-stained khakis and workshoes spattered with white dust
from a building site. An inch-thick circle of black sock shows.
What's life inside those rooms, soup spoiling the air with fat,
everyone always almost touching, touching, always hearing each
other, TV snoring away, emanating its trustful blue glow? It took
at least an hour, riding through that neighborhood, on the street
between slum and near-slum, to reach the bike shop in Chestnut
Hill, its main street jammed with Shoppes, colonial facades in
yellow, putty and green, their windows crammed with cheeses,
garden tools, skis, crystal, imported wool, the cobbled streets as clean
as country roads. Millie and I were going to the Hill Cycle Shop to
pick out our daughter's Christmas gift, a 10-speed bike. We chatted
on the way, watched people stepping off, and on, marvelled at how
far over on a curve the trolley would lean and not topple, at the
crookedness of the track that would jerk the car and clack it to one
side then pop it back straight as it wobbled on its route uphill
through dilapidated shopping districts—Black, Irish, Polish—past
handmade cardboard signs and cars with For Sale signs, a phone
number taped on a window, old clothes and furniture, spackling in
cracks and blob-shaped patches chipped off, a world used hard and
long where nobody ever had time to stop, to let it rest, to fix or

refurbish. At one point along the way two fat white wives of blue-collar workers got on and sat behind us, their hair was dyed pale blue oyster white, cut short, curled, sprayed stiff as cocoons. Their skin shone like a bar of margarine, a clean scent flared from them, indistinct, vapid, renunciatory, sweet, like the smell that hits you when you enter a dime store. For blocks there was silence, the monotony of watching defunct bare stores—a wing chair stuck in a window, a checked wrinkled summer jacket flung down, a faded sleeve, salt and pepper shakers, ashtrays, one marble with a chrome-dipped naked nymph, arms up, perched on the edge—things drifted to the edge of existence, futility in things. A tall skinny black kid bops up the steps into the car, stands, ass tilted against a pole, one of those massive plastic and chrome boom-boxes slung on his shoulder, all three speakers blaring. A few blocks later the doors flap apart and he slips off into the street and I hear one of the women behind us in a low voice telling her friend a story: "I don't know why... my niece, Kathy, killed herself with pills... there's this clinic around the corner from me and I decided to go there, get a doctor, something was scaring me after Kathy, and I'm sitting in his office, I guess it's the third visit, just him and me, and he asks me about my sex life, do you believe it? How often do I have sex? So I blasted him, I said, 'I'll be goddamned if I'll tell a complete stranger about something like that . . .' and walked out and never went back." Her niece—all that promise, all that lust of excitement and touch, of being entered and held, youth blowing loneliness away, intimacy, orgasm, the first taste of the holiness of pleasure—it must have been sacrilege for a member of that family, its morality strict as a stoplight, to kill herself. It must have seemed criminal for someone to connect the death with sex. Then silence. Now, brooding on silence, on a lost unfulfilled soul, on puberty, on poverty's unheal-able wound, on the soul's incomprehensible necessity of openness to soul, I know we can't own anything, can't depend on anything, believe in anything, escape anything. Millie and I glanced at each other but we didn't speak. The two women said nothing either after that tirade, after one blurted her meager worrisome details, clues to the whole tale. Often that's where I am: in the silence of the unexplained that falls after someone has told heartfelt killing facts connected to the unspeakable, to unlived life, so an entire family's invisible connections seem suddenly to pluck the air and hum, piercing, unclear. You feel the need to understand and speak to the person who spoke in the seat behind you, maybe that would offer hope. What can a stranger give to a stranger? A story of his own, one of those incidents of love, lost love, the unending quest to define love? Maybe I should have gotten up and taken the seat behind them—it was empty—leaned close to their heads and whispered a consolation, anything, what a father might say to his daughter who's come to him and sits in silence, one evening, wrought with anxiety, afraid to discuss the facts behind her pain. "Listen," I might have said, leaning close, "I know what you mean. There's a part of life I never seem able to live, or can't live as fully as I need to, it's hard to explain, but when someone suffers and tells you about it it's as if that part of me I can't make live might die forever in the other person's pain right then . . . aren't we all looking for the love that helps us to enter . . . 'this dark region within ourselves, which is at once dark for us and dark for others and can only be illuminated for ourselves in trying to illuminate it for others' . . . you see, the thing is, all this searching, wondering, it doesn't get you out of your life, you're always in your life, and it's true—we're so mortal God can put His hand through us as if we were air, speaking air, poor fleshless images suspended in air." We reach our stop, still silent, get off, walk a block, find the bike shop window. The noon sun arches behind us. I press my face to the cold, clean glass—inside out, outside in—listening as the glass listens. No need to speak. Trucks, voices, scufflings buzz on the window, against my face. I move my head back, about an inch, toward the stable world behind us in the street, our two transparent faces in front of us on the pane bodiless, as they were before we were, and as they will be, the self-erasing, world-erasing light bathing us the way a mother dips her infant, gently, bit by bit, into its warm bath.

If you knew where suffering comes from, if you could fathom that one last fraction of its source, the root tip that seems unreachable, mystical, wouldn't you starve just to see it, talk to it, hold it between your hands, shield it, let it be heard, isn't it the one thing you'd rather know than anything—where the dread comes from when it seeps into your belly and chest, into you, like a stink you hit driving the turnpike—skunk, pig shit, chemicals—or like one's poor conscience crying *No! No! You can't do that, can't say that.* You believe the "you" you are might even disappear if you act, speak, begin to reveal what's there, wherever "there" is, whatever "it" is that wants and does not want to be heard. Some still call it the soul but it's what we know about ourselves that's trapped inside us, what Sartre calls the "depth of darkness" in us. Some mornings you get up needing to share the "dark region" that can "only be illuminated for ourselves in trying to illuminate it for others." You sit at your desk, sip coffee: thoughts, traces of comprehension, images, evaporate: you flip through books in stacks already gnawed at, underlined, page after page, look out the window, try more books—"A man's existence must be entirely visible to his neighbor, whose own existence must be entirely visible in turn, before true social harmony can be established." — you type—background of birds and traffic—and look outside again as the voices inside you you wish would speak fade and go silent. Titles on spines. Page edges. "When once the truth is grasped that one's own personality is only a ridiculous and aimless masquerade of something hopelessly unknown, the attainment of serenity is not very far off," Conrad says in one of his letters on life and art. In Princeton once, I drifted through the library into the rare books wing and saw every book he wrote, first editions standing on edge or propped on wire easels, some closed flat on their backs in glass cases or lined up on shelves, some spread open with ribbon to the frontispiece—his prissy Van Dyck beard and narrow sorrowful puzzled black eyes stare, a high white collar propping up his chin, his suit jacket's buttoned to the last, top button, almost to the neck. What an incongruous formal figure he cuts in those photos and lithos when you think of the pain in his books, his relentlessly etched landscapes, his disheveled tortured men being peeled away until they see themselves, abandoned to the abyss of mind, of self, of nature, to "truth stripped of its cloak of time," suspicion worming out their brains, all substance charred in the fires of moral possibility, a maze-like gloom suffusing the earth. ". . . the rescued fragment . . ." is a phrase from one of his essays that haunts me. "The task approached in tenderness and faith is to hold up unquestionably, without choice and without fear, the rescued fragment before all eyes in the light of a sincere mood." Or Stein to Marlowe: "How to be! . . . We want in so many ways to be." or ". . . another man's infinite need . . ." and how ". . .to grapple with it." "Needed rather than needing" An old friend calls it in a letter to me: "One night while I was waiting for my wife to come out of the bathroom so I could start the porno movie, I was flipping the channels and came to a broadcast of the Hasid Convention in New York, some big special thing when the Hasids from all over the world come to hear the head Rabbi speak. I was stoned, sort of drifting, watching it, they were all from some other epoch, bearded, hats, chanting something, and there was a voice-over that must have been translating the Rabbi's sermon, and it said something that really struck me, something, I don't remember in what context, human or divine, but I took it to mean human, about being needed rather than needing . . ." He wrote that to me after a time on the phone spent talking to the point where each of us heard the other the way a mother goes to its infant's cry and lays her face against its face in love that needs nothing for itself, that has no self, that hears the very center of the child's anxiety so it knows it and can sleep. The restrained tenderness in every copy of Conrad's face, the dignity in his fear of love, the heavy-lidded Oriental eyes and thin mouth, felt alive. He and I, alone in the silent room. Some of the books showed a page he had dedicated and signed. One case held six full-face portraits, all with that rigid collar crowding his chin, nothing suggesting jungle, ships or oceans. I strolled around, stopping, looking, reading whenever I saw a page of text or a letter. From not one etching or photo does he look straight ahead out at you so you feel he is looking at *you*, his eyes stray off to the left or right, half-shut, scouring blank distance that extends forever like the surface of the sea, poised, waiting to hear someone, you perhaps, speak and expect an answer, speak in the fullness of his need.

Lately that's how it's been for me, living in the wish, hearing it inflect the late night silence often like isolated street noise so clear it isn't simply a voice recurring but a steady gentle whisper next to my ear—*I want to die now* or *Please let me die, okay?* That's how my father must have felt the night of his last, massive heart attack: so weary, wanting it because it was the only way he could solve himself. I was told he gulped down two quart cans of Campbell's tomato juice, went back to bed, then woke with chest pain, jaw pain, pain down his arm, stumbled to the kitchen and vomited until the ambulance my mother called came and took him off, unconscious. Then the delirium in ICU, tubes and monitors, two weeks of raving he's on a plane to Miami captured by the Nazis; then back to life; sitting in bed, real food, TV, and finally, miraculously, home, the family calling, visiting, waiting, the air each day seared a little by the peril of this dying man, this father, this origin who should share some kind of wisdom before he dies, but can't. The nice thing is it can give survivors a kind of passionate secret song to try when they can't say where their pain's coming from, why their lives are the way they are, how and what to change, a song of infinite consolation, it probably seems, much much deeper than grief. It doesn't have words or sounds you can actually modulate with lips and teeth and tongue, like a song. It comes by itself at odd times when you've stopped thinking, are sure you never want to be touched again, wonder who caused what and why. Your mouth opens. You can't tell whose lips move. Your face in the darkness breathes. Space breathes. Like that luminous gray wall in the Vermeer—a young woman sits at a table or a desk, turned toward us, toward a maid who's handing her a letter. The expression on her face—cautiously poised, veiled apprehension, not quite fear—says what's inside the envelope could change the placid room, her placid life, instantaneously, by igniting the straw of pain that's always susceptible to a treacherous fact or the scope of another's will or unearned unavoid-able bad news. Behind her, soaked in mellow pearly light, the wall looks like the light is welling out of it, though a window fills the left edge of the painting. The wall seems one solid yet absolutely ephemeral plane the viewer or the woman could pass through without the least effort. That's it—it's a zone of grace and silence, a holiness of pure color, safe, fair and unconcerned, endlessly itself, the place we look for in ourselves as the source of faith, the always accessible otherness that is not personal or even human. And, yes, it breathes like your face in a room on one of those hard nights when thought exhausts itself. Lying alone, seeing it, you want to kiss the wall, then lean all of yourself against it, run your hands across its fine-grained, plaster skin, warm with sun, then press your cheek to its huge body, shut your eyes, stay.

Stephen Berg's books of poetry include *The Daughters, Grief: Poems and Versions of Poems, With Akhmatova at the Black Gates, In It, Crow with No Mouth: Ikkyū, Homage to the Afterlife, New & Selected Poems, Oblivion,* and *The Steel Cricket: Versions 1958-1997.* He is the translator of *Oedipus The King* (with Diskin Clay), and Miklós Radnóti's book of anti-Fascist poems *Clouded Sky* (with Steven Polgar & S.J. Marks). He has received Guggenheim, NEA, Ford, Rockefeller, Dietrich, and Pew Fellowships, *Poetry* magazine's Frank O'Hara Memorial Prize, and is founder and co-editor of *The American Poetry Review.*